BEATLES

Cover photo: Michael Ochs Archives/Venice, CA

A POCKET REFERENCE GUIDE TO MORE THAN 100 SONGS!

HAL•LEONARD

Copyright © 1995 by HAL LEONARD CORPORATION
International Copyright Secured   All Rights Reserved

For all works contained herein:
Unauthorized copying, arranging, adapting, recording or public
performance is an infringement of copyright.
Infringers are liable under the law.

This publication is not for sale in
the E.C. and/or Australia
or New Zealand.

HAL•LEONARD™
CORPORATION

7777 W. BLUEMOUND RD. P.O. BOX 13819 MILWAUKEE, WI 53213

Welcome to the PAPERBACK SONGS SERIES.

Do you play piano, guitar, electronic keyboard, sing or play any instrument for that matter? If so, this handy "pocket tune" book is for you.

The concise, one-line music notation consists of:

MELODY, LYRICS & CHORD SYMBOLS

Whether strumming the chords on guitar, "faking" an arrangement on piano/keyboard or singing the lyrics, these fake book style arrangements can be enjoyed at any experience level – hobbyist to professional.

The musical skills necessary to successfully use this book are minimal. If you play guitar and need some help with chords, a basic chord chart is included at the back of the book.

While playing and singing is the first thing that comes to mind when using this book, it can also serve as a compact, comprehensive reference guide.

However you choose to use this PAPERBACK SONGS SERIES book, by all means have fun!

CONTENTS

ACROSS THE UNIVERSE

Words and Music by
JOHN LENNON and PAUL McCARTNEY

Slowly, and smoothly

Words are flow-ing out_ like end-less rain_ in-to a pa-per cup,_ they

slith-er while_ they pass, they slip a-way_ A-cross The U-ni-verse._

Pools of sor-row, waves of joy are drift-ing through my o-pened mind,_ pos-

sess-ing and ca-ress-ing me._

Jai_ Gu-ru_ De-va. Om._

Noth-ing's gon-na change my world,_

Noth-ing's gon-na change my world._

© 1968, 1970 NORTHERN SONGS LTD.
All Rights Controlled and Administered by EMI BLACKWOOD MUSIC INC.
under license from ATV MUSIC CORP. (MACLEN MUSIC)

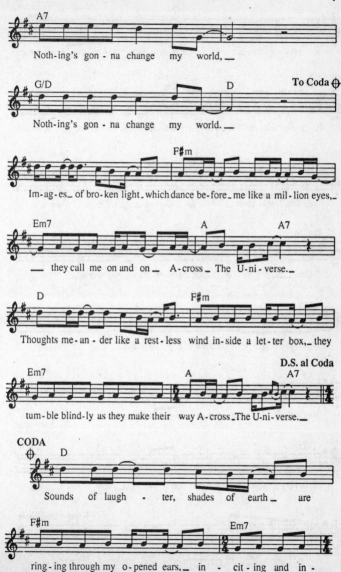

AND YOUR BIRD CAN SING

Words and Music by
JOHN LENNON and PAUL McCARTNEY

Moderately

(Instrumental)

Tell me that you've got ev-'ry-thing you want,
You say you've seen sev-en won-ders,

And Your Bird Can Sing, but you don't get me,—
and your bird is green, but you can't see me,—

you don't get me.
you don't get me.

1.

2.
When your prized — pos-ses-
When your bird — is bro-

© 1966 NORTHERN SONGS LTD.
All Rights Controlled and Administered by EMI BLACKWOOD MUSIC INC.
under license from ATV MUSIC CORP. (MACLEN MUSIC)

G+   Bm/F#

- sions   start   to   weigh_ you   down,
- ken.   Will   it   bring_ you   down?_

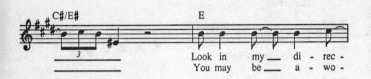

C#/E#   E

Look   in   my_ di - rec -
You may   be_ a - wo -

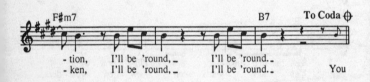

F#m7   B7   To Coda ⊕

- tion,   I'll be 'round, _   I'll be 'round._
- ken,   I'll be 'round, _   I'll be 'round._   You

E

(Instrumental)

F#m7

B7   E   D.S. al Coda

11

CODA

tell me that you've heard ev - 'ry sound there is,

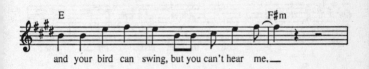

and your bird can swing, but you can't hear me,___

You can't hear   me.   *(Instrumental)*

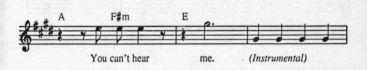

ALL MY LOVING

Words and Music by
JOHN LENNON and PAUL McCARTNEY

© 1963, 1964 NORTHERN SONGS LTD.
Copyright Renewed
All Rights Controlled and Administered by EMI BLACKWOOD MUSIC INC.
under license from ATV MUSIC CORP. (MACLEN MUSIC)

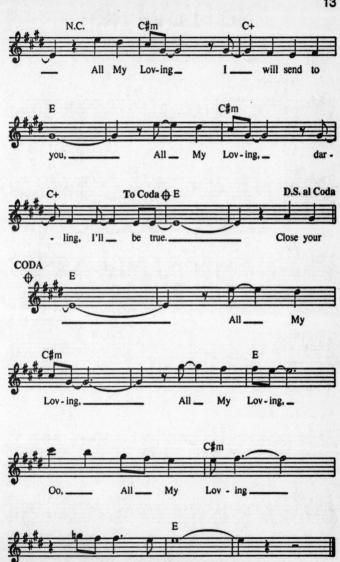

AND I LOVE HER

Words and Music by
JOHN LENNON and PAUL McCARTNEY

© 1964 NORTHERN SONGS LTD.
Copyright Renewed
All Rights Controlled and Administered by EMI BLACKWOOD MUSIC INC.
under license from ATV MUSIC CORP. (MACLEN MUSIC)

have you near me.

CODA

Instrumental ad lib.
Bright are the stars

that shine, dark is the sky.

I know this love of mine will nev-er die,

And I Love Her.

Her. *(Instrumental)*

ALL YOU NEED IS LOVE

Words and Music by
JOHN LENNON and PAUL McCARTNEY

(Instrumental)

Love   love   love   love   love

love   Love   love   love

(Instrumental)

There's noth-ing you can do   that can't be done.___
There's noth-ing you can make that can't be made.___
There's noth-ing you can know that is-n't known.___

Noth-ing you can sing   that can't be sung.___
No- one you can save   that can't be saved.___
Noth-ing you can see   that isn't shown.___

Noth-ing   you can say   but you can learn _ how to play the game.
Noth-ing   you can do   but you can learn _ how to be you in time   } It's
No-where you can be   that is-n't where _ you're meant to be.___

© 1967 NORTHERN SONGS LTD.
All Rights Controlled and Administered by EMI BLACKWOOD MUSIC INC.
under license from ATV MUSIC CORP. (MACLEN MUSIC)

18

BIRTHDAY

Words and Music by
JOHN LENNON and PAUL McCARTNEY

You say it's your Birth - day,   It's
my Birth-day too,_ yeah;   They say it's your Birth - day,

© 1968 NORTHERN SONGS LTD.
All Rights Controlled and Administered by EMI BLACKWOOD MUSIC INC.
under license from ATV MUSIC CORP. (MACLEN MUSIC)

We're gon-na have a good time; I'm glad it's your Birth - day, Hap - py Birth - day to ___ you.

Yse, we're go - in' to a par - ty, par - ty,

Yes, we're go - in' to a par - ty, par - ty,

Yes, we're go - in to a par - ty, par - ty.

I would like you to dance, ___

(Birth - day) ___ Take a cha - cha - cha - chance, ___

(Birth - day) __ I would like you to dance, __

(Birth - day) __ Dance! __

To Coda ⊕

(Instrumental)

D.S. al Coda

CODA
⊕ A7

You say it's your Birth - day,

D7

It's my Birth-day too, __ yeah; They

A7

say it's your Birth - day. We're gon-na have a good time;

E7   A7

I'm glad it's your Birth - day, Hap-py

Birth-day to __ you. *(Instrumental)*

BABY, YOU'RE
A RICH MAN

Words and Music by
JOHN LENNON and PAUL McCARTNEY

How does it feel to be one of the beau-ti-ful peo-ple Now that you know who you are what do you want to be And have you trav-elled ver-y far far as the eye can see How does it feel to be one of the beau-ti-ful peo-ple

How of-ten have you been there
Tuned to a nat-ur-al E

© 1967 NORTHERN SONGS LTD.
All Rights Controlled and Administered by EMI BLACKWOOD MUSIC INC.
under license from ATV MUSIC CORP. (MACLEN MUSIC)

BACK IN THE U.S.S.R.

Words and Music by
JOHN LENNON and PAUL McCARTNEY

Moderate Rock

Flew in from Mi-a-mi Beach, B. O. A. C., __ Did __
Been a-way so long I hard-ly knew the place, __ Gee __
Show me 'round your snow-peaked moun-tains way down south, __ Take __

__ n't get to bed last night. __ On __
__ it's good to get back home. __ Leave __
__ me to your dad-dy's farm. __ Let __

__ the way the pa-per bag was on my knee, __ Man __
__ it till to-mor-row to un-pack my case, __ Hon- __
__ me hear your bal-a-lai-kas ring-ing out, __ Come __

__ I had a dread-ful flight. __
-ey, dis-con-nect the phone. } I'm Back In The U. S. S. R., __
__ and keep your com-rade warm. __

__ You don't __ know how luck-y you are, __

To Coda ⊕
1.
boy. __ Back In The U. S. S. R.

2.
Back In The U. S.

© 1968 NORTHERN SONGS LTD.
All Rights Controlled and Administered by EMI BLACKWOOD MUSIC INC.
under license from ATV MUSIC CORP. (MACLEN MUSIC)

THE BALLAD OF JOHN AND YOKO

Words and Music by
JOHN LENNON and PAUL McCARTNEY

Moderate Rock

1. Stand-ing in the dock at South-amp - ton,
2. Final - ly made the plane in - to Pa - ris,
3. Pa - ris to the Am-ster-dam Hil - ton,

trying to get to Hol-land or France.__ The
hon - ey-moon-ing down by the Seine. __ Pe - ter
talk - ing in our beds for a week. __ The

man in the mac__ said__ "You've got to go back." You know they
Brown called to say, "You__ can make it O.K., ___ You can get
news - peo-ple said, "Say what're you do-ing in bed?"_ I said, "We're

did - n't e - ven give us a chance._ ⎫
mar - ried in Gib - ral - ter near Spain." _ ⎬ Christ! You know it ain't eas -
on - ly trying to get us some peace." _ ⎭

- y, ___ you know how hard it can be. __

The way things are go -

© 1969 NORTHERN SONGS LTD.
All Rights Controlled and Administered by EMI BLACKWOOD MUSIC INC.
under license from ATV MUSIC CORP. (MACLEN MUSIC)

- ing ___ they're gon - na cru - ci - fy ___

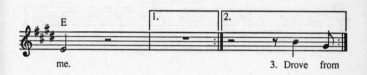

me.

1.

2.

3. Drove from

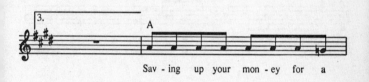

3.

Sav - ing up your mon - ey for a

rain - y day, ___ giv-ing all your clothes to char - i

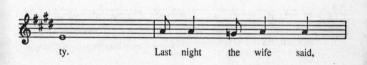

ty. Last night the wife said,

"Oh boy, when you're dead you don't take noth-ing with you but your

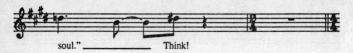

soul." _____ Think!

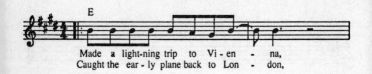

Made a light-ning trip to Vi-en - na,
Caught the ear-ly plane back to Lon - don,

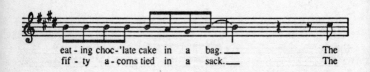

eat-ing choc-'late cake in a bag. ___   The
fif-ty a-corns tied in a sack. ___   The

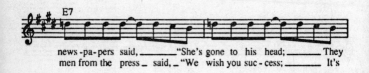

news-pa-pers said, _____ "She's gone to his head; _____ They
men from the press _ said, _ "We wish you suc-cess; _____ It's

look just like two Gu-rus in drag." _ } Christ! You know it ain't eas -
good to have the both of you back." _ }

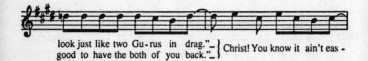

- y,   you know how hard it can be. ___

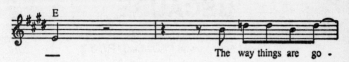

The way things are go -

- ing ____ they're going to cru - ci - fy ____

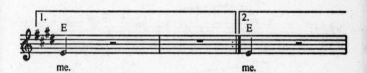

1.
me.

2.
me.

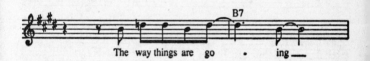

The way things are go - ing ____

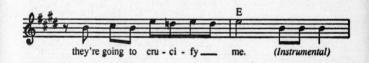

they're going to cru - ci - fy ____ me. *(Instrumental)*

BECAUSE

Words and Music by
JOHN LENNON and PAUL McCARTNEY

Moderately slow

(Instrumental)

Ah, _____

_____ Be - cause the world is round, it turns me
cause the wind is high, it blows my
cause the sky is blue, it makes me

on: _____ Be - cause _____ the
mind; _____ Be - cause _____ the
cry; _____ Be - cause _____ the

world is round. _____
wind is high. _____
sky is blue. _____

To Coda ⊕

© 1969 NORTHERN SONGS LTD.
All Rights Controlled and Administered by EMI BLACKWOOD MUSIC INC.
under license from ATV MUSIC CORP. (MACLEN MUSIC)

31

BEING FOR THE BENEFIT OF MR. KITE

Words and Music by
JOHN LENNON and PAUL McCARTNEY

For the ben-e-fit ___ of Mis-ter Kite,
cel-e-brat-ed Mis-ter K., per-
band be-gins ___ at ten to six when

there will be ___ a show to-night on tram-po-line.
from his feat ___ on Sat-ur-day at Bish-ops-gate.
Mis-ter K. ___ per-forms his tricks with-out a sound.

The Hen-der-sons will all be there,
The Hen-der-sons will dance and sing as
And Mis-ter H. will dem-on-strate ten

late of Pab-lo Fan-que's fair; what a scene. ___ O-ver
Mis-ter Kite flies through the ring; don't be late. ___ Mes-s'rs
som-er-sets he'll un-der-take on sol-id ground. ___ Hav-ing

© 1967 NORTHERN SONGS LTD.
All Rights Controlled and Administered by EMI BLACKWOOD MUSIC INC.
under license from ATV MUSIC CORP. (MACLEN MUSIC)

33

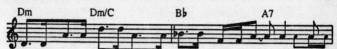

men and hors-es, hoops and gat - ters, last - ly through a hog's head of
K. and H. as-sure the pub - lic their pro - duc-tion will _ be sec-ond to
been some days in prep- a - ra-tion, a splen-did time is guar - an-teed for

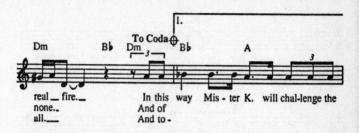

To Coda⊕   1.

real _ fire. _   In this way Mis - ter K. will chal-lenge the
none. _   And of
all. _   And to-

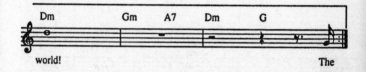

world!   The

2.

course, Hen-ry, The Horse, danc-es the   waltz!

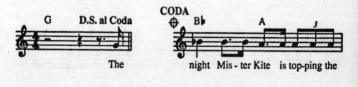

G   D.S. al Coda   CODA⊕

            The   night Mis - ter Kite is top-ping the

bill.   (Instrumental)

BLACKBIRD

Words and Music by
JOHN LENNON and PAUL McCARTNEY

Slowly and smoothly

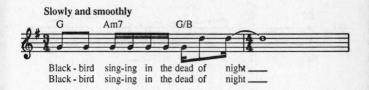

Black - bird sing-ing in the dead of night ___
Black - bird sing-ing in the dead of night ___

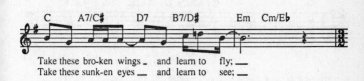

Take these bro-ken wings _ and learn to fly; ___
Take these sunk-en eyes _ and learn to see; ___

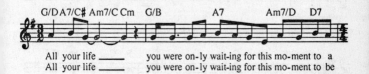

All your life ___ you were on-ly wait-ing for this mo-ment to a
All your life ___ you were on-ly wait-ing for this mo-ment to be

rise. *(Instrumental)*

free. Black - bird, ___ fly, ___

© 1968, 1969 NORTHERN SONGS LTD.
All Rights Controlled and Administered by EMI BLACKWOOD MUSIC INC.
under license from ATV MUSIC CORP. (MACLEN MUSIC)

F C/E Dm C   Bb   A7

Black - bird, ___   fly, _____   in - to the

D7   G   Am7   G/B

light   of   a   dark,   black   night. ___

G   C A7/C# D7 B7/D#   Em   Cm/Eb

(Instrumental)

Gmaj7/D A7/C# Am7/C Cm   G/B   A7   D7   G

F C/E Dm C   Bb   C   F C/E Dm C

Black - bird, ___   fly, ___   Black - bird, ___   fly, ___

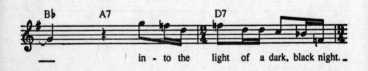

Bb   A7   D7

___   in - to the   light of a dark, black night. ___

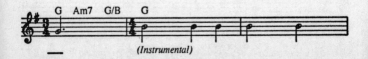

G   Am7 G/B   G

___   *(Instrumental)*

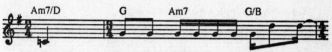

Black-bird sing-ing in the dead of night ＿

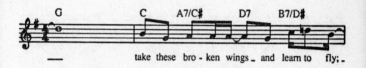

＿ take these bro-ken wings ＿ and learn to fly; ＿

＿ All your life ＿＿＿＿＿

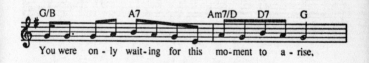

You were on-ly wait-ing for this mo-ment to a-rise,

You were on-ly wait-ing for this mo-ment to a-rise.

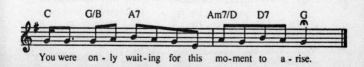

You were on-ly wait-ing for this mo-ment to a-rise.

COME TOGETHER

Words and Music by
JOHN LENNON and PAUL McCARTNEY

Moderately slow, with a double time feeling

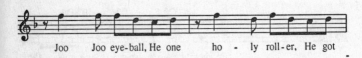

Here come old flat-top, He come   groov - ing up slow-ly, He got

Joo   Joo eye-ball, He one   ho - ly roll-er, He got

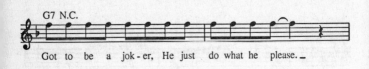

hair   down   to   his   knee. ___

Got to be a jok - er, He just do what he please. ___

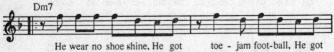

He wear no shoe shine, He got   toe - jam foot-ball, He got
He Bag Pro-duc - tion, He got   wal - rus gum-boot, He got
He roll - er coast - er, He got   ear - ly warn-ing, He got

© 1969 NORTHERN SONGS LTD.
All Rights Controlled and Administered by EMI BLACKWOOD MUSIC INC.
under license from ATV MUSIC CORP. (MACLEN MUSIC)

CAN'T BUY ME LOVE

Words and Music by
JOHN LENNON and PAUL McCARTNEY

© 1964 NORTHERN SONGS LTD.
Copyright Renewed
All Rights Controlled and Administered by EMI BLACKWOOD MUSIC INC.
under license from ATV MUSIC CORP. (MACLEN MUSIC)

DAY TRIPPER

Words and Music by
JOHN LENNON and PAUL McCARTNEY

Moderate Rock

N.C.

(Instrumental)

E7

Got a good rea - son for
She's a big teas - er,
Tried to please her,

tak - ing the eas - y way out, ___
she took me half ___ the way there. ___
she on - ly played ___ one-night stands. ___

A7

Got a good rea - son for
She's a big teas - er,
Tried to please her,

© 1965 NORTHERN SONGS LTD.
Copyright Renewed
All Rights Controlled and Administered by EMI BLACKWOOD MUSIC INC.
under license from ATV MUSIC CORP. (MACLEN MUSIC)

B7   E/B   F#m/B

Ah _____

B6   A/B   B7   **D.C. al Coda**

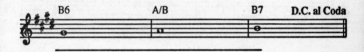

CODA

B   N.C.

out.   *(Instrumental)*

Play 3 times

Repeat and Fade

E7

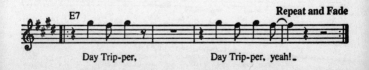

Day Trip-per,   Day Trip-per, yeah!

A DAY IN THE LIFE

Words and Music by
JOHN LENNON and PAUL McCARTNEY

Slowly

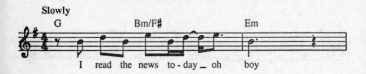

I read the news to-day _ oh boy

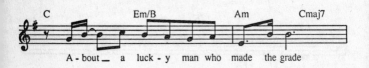

A - bout _ a luck - y man who made the grade

And though the news _ was rath - er sad

Well I just had to laugh _____

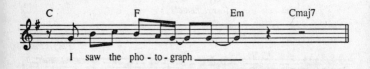

I saw the pho - to - graph _____

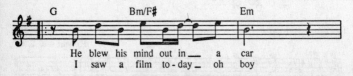

He blew his mind out in __ a car
I saw a film to - day _ oh boy

© 1967 NORTHERN SONGS LTD.
All Rights Controlled and Administered by EMI BLACKWOOD MUSIC INC.
under license from ATV MUSIC CORP. (MACLEN MUSIC)

He did-n't no-tice that the lights had changed.
The Eng-lish ar-my had just won the war.

A crowd of peo-ple stood and stared   They'd seen his face be-fore
A crowd of peo-ple turned a-way   But I just had to look

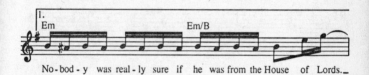

1.
Em

No-bod-y was real-ly sure if he was from the House of Lords.

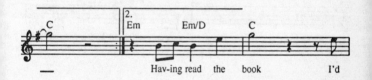

2.
Em   Em/D   C

Hav-ing read the book   I'd

love to turn   you   on.

(Instrumental)   Woke up.

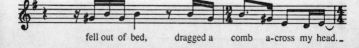

fell out of bed,   dragged a comb a-cross my head.

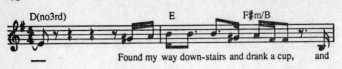

Found my way down-stairs and drank a cup, and

look-ing up I no-ticed I was late. Found my

coat and grabbed my hat_ made the bus in sec-onds

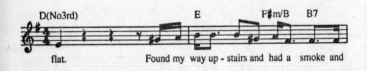

flat. Found my way up-stairs and had a smoke and

some-bod-y spoke and I went in-to a dream. Ah____

DON'T LET ME DOWN

Words and Music by
JOHN LENNON and PAUL McCARTNEY

Slowly

(Instrumental) Don't Let Me Down,

Don't Let Me Down. __ Don't Let Me

Down. __ Don't Let Me Down. __

{ No - bod - y ev - er loved me like she does oo she
and from the first time that she real - ly done me, oo she

does, ____ yes, she does.
done ____ me, she done good.

And if some - bod - y loved me like she do me, oo she
I guess no - bod - y ev - er real - ly done me, oo she

© 1969 NORTHERN SONGS LTD.
All Rights Controlled and Administered by EMI BLACKWOOD MUSIC INC.
under license from ATV MUSIC CORP. (MACLEN MUSIC)

DRIVE MY CAR

Words and Music by
JOHN LENNON and PAUL McCARTNEY

Moderately, with a beat

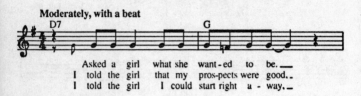

Asked a girl what she want-ed to be.___
I told the girl that my pros-pects were good.___
I told the girl I could start right a - way,___

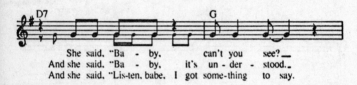

She said, "Ba - by, can't you see?___
And she said, "Ba - by, it's un - der - stood.___
And she said, "Lis-ten, babe, I got some-thing to say.

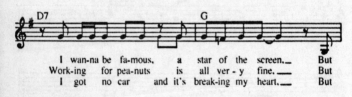

I wan-na be fa-mous, a star of the screen.___ But
Work-ing for pea-nuts is all ver-y fine.___ But
I got no car and it's break-ing my heart.___ But

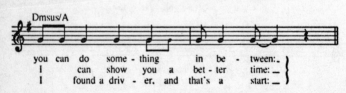

you can do some-thing in be - tween:___
I can show you a bet - ter time:___
I found a driv - er, and that's a start:___

"Ba - by, you can Drive My Car.___

© 1965 NORTHERN SONGS LTD.
Copyright Renewed
All Rights Controlled and Administered by EMI BLACKWOOD MUSIC INC.
under license from ATV MUSIC CORP. (MACLEN MUSIC)

Yes, I'm gon - na be a star, ___

Ba - by, you can Drive My Car, ___ and may - be I'll love ___

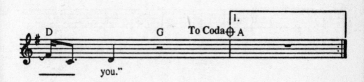

___ you."

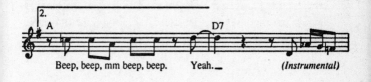

Beep, beep, mm beep, beep. Yeah. ___ *(Instrumental)*

"Ba - by, you can Drive My Car, ___

Yes, I'm gon - na be a star, ___

Ba - by, you can Drive My Car, ___ and may - be I'll love_

___ ___ you."

CODA

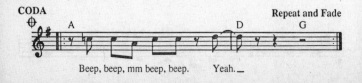

Beep, beep, mm beep, beep. Yeah. ___

EIGHT DAYS A WEEK

Words and Music by
JOHN LENNON and PAUL McCARTNEY

Brightly, with a Swing feel

Ooh I need your love, babe, _
Love you ev - 'ry day, girl, _

guess you know it's true, _
al - ways on my mind. _

Hope you need my love, babe, _
One thing I can say, girl, _

just like I need you. _ }
love you all the time. _ }

Hold me, _ love me, _ Hold me, _

love me. _ I ain't got noth - in' but

© 1964 NORTHERN SONGS LTD.
Copyright Renewed
All Rights Controlled and Administered by EMI BLACKWOOD MUSIC INC.
under license from ATV MUSIC CORP. (MACLEN MUSIC)

ELEANOR RIGBY

Words and Music by
JOHN LENNON and PAUL McCARTNEY

Moderately, with a steady beat

Ah _____ look at all _____ the lone - ly peo - ple! _____ *(Instrumental)*

Ah _____ look at all _____ the lone - ly peo - ple! _____ *(Instrumental)*

El - ea - nor Rig - by, picks up the rice _____ in the church _____ where a wed - ding has been, _____ lives in a dream. _____ Waits at the win - dow,

Fa - ther Mc Ken - zie, writ-ing the words _____ of a ser - mon that no _____ one will hear, _____ no one comes near. _____ Look at him work - ing,

El - ea - nor Rig - by, died in the church _____ and was bur - ied a - long _____ with her name, _____ no - bod - y came. _____ Fa - ther Mc Ken - zie,

© 1966 NORTHERN SONGS LTD.
Copyright Renewed
All Rights Controlled and Administered by EMI BLACKWOOD MUSIC INC.
under license from ATV MUSIC CORP. (MACLEN MUSIC)

wear - ing the face _ that she keeps _ in a jar _ by the door, _
damp - ing his socks _ in the night _ when there's no - bod - y there, _
wip - ing the dirt _ from his hands _ as he walks _ from the grave, _

C   Em

_   who   is   it   for? _____
_   what does he   care? _____
_   no   one   was   saved. _____

Em7   Em6

All   the lone - ly peo - ple,   where do _

C/E   Em

_   they   all _____   come   from? _

Em7   Em6

All   the lone - ly peo - ple,   where do _

                              To Coda ⊕
C/E   Em

_   they   all _____   be - long? _

2.
Em   D. S. al Coda   CODA
                            ⊕   Em

_

EVERY LITTLE THING

Words and Music by
JOHN LENNON and PAUL McCARTNEY

Moderately

When I'm walk-ing be-side her,
I re-mem-ber the first time,

Peo-ple tell me I'm luck-y.
I was lone-ly with-out___ her.

Yes, I know I'm a luck-y guy.___
Yes, I'm think-ing a-bout her now.___

Ev-'ry Lit-tle Thing she does,

she does for me,___ yeah.___ And you know the

things she does, she does for me,___ ooh.___

When I'm with her I'm hap-py
There is one thing I'm sure of

© 1964 NORTHERN SONGS LTD.
Copyright Renewed
All Rights Controlled and Administered by EMI BLACKWOOD MUSIC INC.
under license from ATV MUSIC CORP. (MACLEN MUSIC)

FIXING A HOLE

Words and Music by
JOHN LENNON and PAUL McCARTNEY

© 1967 NORTHERN SONGS LTD.
All Rights Controlled and Administered by EMI BLACKWOOD MUSIC INC.
under license from ATV MUSIC CORP. (MACLEN MUSIC)

63

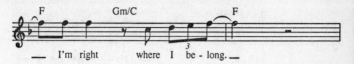

I'm right where I be - long. __

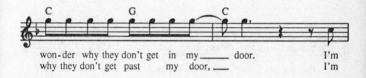

See the peo - ple stand- ing there __ who dis-a gree _ and nev-er win and
Sil - ly peo - ple run _ a - round, who wor-ry me __ and nev-er ask _ me

won - der why they don't get in my_____ door.   I'm
why they don't get past   my door, __   I'm

paint-ing the room __ in a col - or-ful way,   and
tak - ing the time __ for a num - ber of things,   that

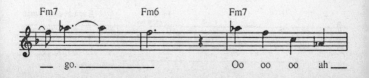

when my mind _ is wan - der-ing   there I will _
weren't im-por - tant yes - ter-day   and I still _

_ go. _____   Oo   oo   oo   ah __

64

And it

CODA

go.

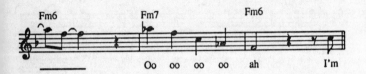

Oo oo oo oo ah I'm

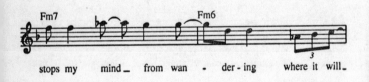

Fix-ing A Hole where the rain gets in, and

stops my mind from wan - der - ing where it will

go, where it will

go. I'm

THE FOOL ON THE HILL

Words and Music by
JOHN LENNON and PAUL McCARTNEY

Slowly

Day af-ter day   A-lone on the hill,___   The
Well on the way,   Head in a cloud,___   The

man with the fool-ish grin is keep-ing per-fect-ly still;   But
man of a thou-sand voic-es talk-ing per-fect-ly loud;   But

no-bod-y wants to know___ him,   They can
no-bod-y ev-er hears___ him,   Or the

see that he's just___ a fool___   And
sound he ap-pears___ to make,___   And

he nev-er gives an an-swer.   But The
he nev-er seems to no-tice.   But The

Fool___ On The Hill___ sees the sun___

© 1967 COMET MUSIC CORP.
All Rights Controlled and Administered by EMI APRIL MUSIC INC.
under license from WELBECK MUSIC CORP. (COMET)

THE FOOL ON THE HILL

Bb/D

go - ing   down __   And   the   eyes __

C

in   his   head __   see   the   world __

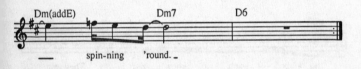

Dm(addE)   **Dm7**   **D6**

spin - ning   'round. _

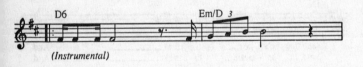

D6   **Em/D** *3*

(Instrumental)

D6   **Em/D**

3   *3*

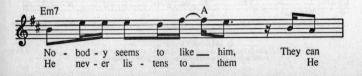

Em7   **A**

No - bod - y   seems   to   like __   him,   They   can
He   nev - er   lis - tens   to __   them   He

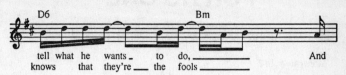

tell what he wants _ to do, ___ And
knows that they're _ the fools ____

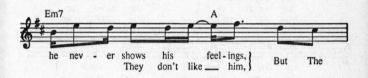

he nev - er shows his feel - ings,
They don't like _ him, } But The

Fool ___ On The Hill _ · sees the sun _

_ go - ing down _ And the eyes _

_ in his head _ see the world _ spin-ning 'round. _

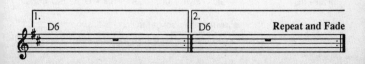

Repeat and Fade

FOR NO ONE

Words and Music by
JOHN LENNON and PAUL McCARTNEY

© 1966 NORTHERN SONGS LTD.
Copyright Renewed
All Rights Controlled and Administered by EMI BLACKWOOD MUSIC INC.
under license from ATV MUSIC CORP. (MACLEN MUSIC)

GET BACK

Words and Music by
JOHN LENNON and PAUL McCARTNEY

Jo Jo was a man who thought he was a lon-er, But
Sweet Lor-et-ta Mar-tin thought she was a wom-an, But

he knew it could-n't last. Jo
she was an-oth-er man. All

Jo left his home in Tuc - son Ar - i - zo - na, for
the girls a-round her say she's got it com-ing, But

some Cal - i - for - nia grass. Get Back!
she gets it while she can. Get Back!

Get Back! Get Back

© 1969 NORTHERN SONGS LTD.
All Rights Controlled and Administered by EMI BLACKWOOD MUSIC INC.
under license from ATV MUSIC CORP. (MACLEN MUSIC)

— to where you once be - longed. _____ Get Back!_

— Get Back! _ Get Back_

— to where you once be - longed. _____ (Get Back, Jo Jo)

— (Instrumental)

Spoken ad lib:

Get Back, Loretta, your momma's waitin' for you
Wearin' her high heel shoes and a low neck sweater.
Get Back home, Loretta.

Repeat and Fade

GETTING BETTER

Words and Music by
JOHN LENNON and PAUL McCARTNEY

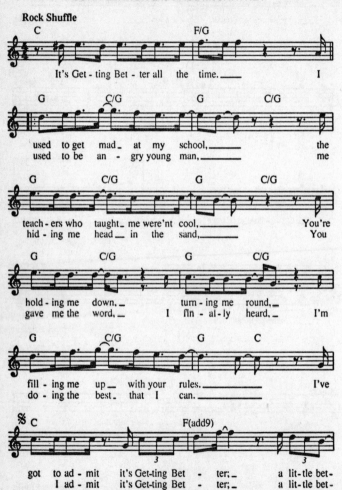

Rock Shuffle

It's Get-ting Bet-ter all the time._____ I

used to get mad at my school,_____ the
used to be an-gry young man,_____ me

teach-ers who taught_ me were'nt cool,_____ You're
hid-ing me head_ in the sand,_____ You

hold-ing me down,_____ turn-ing me round,_____
gave me the word,_ I fin-al-ly heard,_ I'm

fill-ing me up_ with your rules._____ I've
do-ing the best_ that I can._____ I

got to ad-mit it's Get-ting Bet - ter;_ a lit-tle bet-
I ad-mit it's Get-ting Bet - ter;_ a lit-tle bet-

© 1967 NORTHERN SONGS LTD.
All Rights Controlled and Administered by EMI BLACKWOOD MUSIC INC.
under license from ATV MUSIC CORP. (MACLEN MUSIC)

GOT TO GET YOU INTO MY LIFE

Words and Music by
JOHN LENNON and PAUL McCARTNEY

Very steady, with a swing feel

(Instrumental)

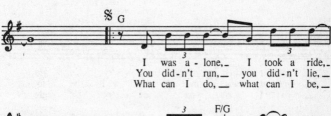

I was a-lone,___ I took a ride,___
You did-n't run,___ you did-n't lie,___
What can I do,___ what can I be,___

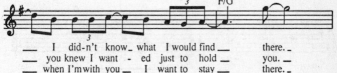

___ I did-n't know___ what I would find ___ there.
___ you knew I want-ed just to hold ___ you. ___
___ when I'm with you ___ I want to stay ___ there.

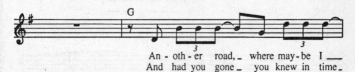

An-oth-er road,___ where may-be I ___
And had you gone___ you knew in time.
If I'm true ___ I'll nev-er leave.

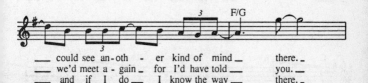

___ could see an-oth-er kind of mind ___ there.
___ we'd meet a-gain for I'd have told ___ you. ___
___ and if I do ___ I know the way ___ there. ___

© 1966 NORTHERN SONGS LTD.
All Rights Controlled and Administered by EMI BLACKWOOD MUSIC INC.
under license from ATV MUSIC CORP. (MACLEN MUSIC)

Ooh, _____ then I sud -
Ooh, _____ you were meant.
Ooh, _____ then I sud -

- den - ly see __ you. Ooh, _____ did I tell __
__ to be near __ me. Ooh, _____ did I want __
- den - ly see __ you. Ooh, _____ did I tell __

__ you I need __ you ev - 'ry sin - gle
__ you to hear __ me say we'll be to -
__ you I need __ you ev - 'ry sin - gle

day of my life? _____
gether ev - 'ry day. _____
day of my life? _____

__ Got To Get You In - to My Life! __

__ *(Instrumental)*

GIRL

Words and Music by
JOHN LENNON and PAUL McCARTNEY

Moderately

Is there an-y-bod-y going to lis-ten to my sto-ry
think of all the times I tried so hard to leave her
told when she was young that pain would lead to plea-sure?

All a-bout the Girl who came to stay? She's the
She will turn to me and start to cry. And she
Did she un-der-stand it when they said That a

kind of Girl you want so much it makes you sor-ry,
prom-is-es the earth to me and I be-lieve her,
man must break his back to earn his day of lei-sure?

Still you don't re-gret a sin-gle day.
Af-ter all this time I don't know why.
Will she still be-lieve it when he's dead? } Ah,

To Coda

Girl, ____

Girl, Girl, ____ When I

She's the kind of Girl who puts you

© 1965 NORTHERN SONGS LTD.
Copyright Renewed
All Rights Controlled and Administered by EMI BLACKWOOD MUSIC INC.
under license from ATV MUSIC CORP. (MACLEN MUSIC)

GOOD DAY SUNSHINE

Words and Music by
JOHN LENNON and PAUL McCARTNEY

Good Day Sun - shine, Good Day Sun -

- shine, Good Day Sun - shine. { I need to
Then we'd

laugh and when the sun is out
lie be - neath a shad - y tree,

I've got some-thing I can laugh a - bout. I feel
I love her and she's lov - ing me. She feels

good in a spe - cial way,
good she knows she's look - ing fine,

I'm in love and it's a sun - ny day.
I'm so proud to know that she is mine.

Good Day Sun - shine, Good Day Sun -

© 1966 NORTHERN SONGS LTD.
Copyright Renewed
All Rights Controlled and Administered by EMI BLACKWOOD MUSIC INC.
under license from ATV MUSIC CORP. (MACLEN MUSIC)

A HARD DAY'S NIGHT

Words and Music by
JOHN LENNON and PAUL McCARTNEY

Moderately, with a beat

© 1964 NORTHERN SONGS LTD.
Copyright Renewed
All Rights Controlled and Administered by EMI BLACKWOOD MUSIC INC.
under license from ATV MUSIC CORP. (MACLEN MUSIC)

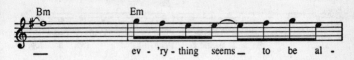

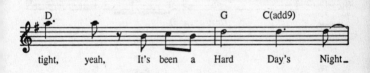

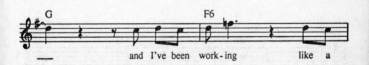

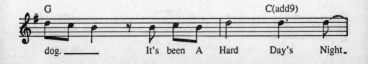

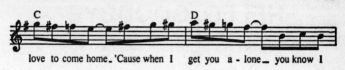

love to come home. 'Cause when I get you a-lone_ you know I

feel_ O._ K._ When I'm home_

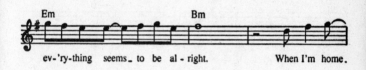

ev-'ry-thing seems_ to be al-right. When I'm home.

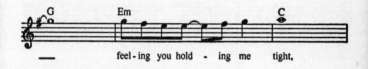

_ feel-ing you hold-ing me tight,

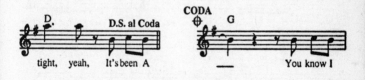

tight, yeah, It's been A

CODA

_ You know I

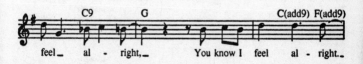

feel_ al-right,_ You know I feel al-right._

Repeat and Fade

_ (Instrumental)

HELLO, GOODBYE

Words and Music by
JOHN LENNON and PAUL McCARTNEY

© 1967 NORTHERN SONGS LTD.
All Rights Controlled and Administered by EMI BLACKWOOD MUSIC INC.
under license from ATV MUSIC CORP. (MACLEN MUSIC)

HERE COMES THE SUN

Words and Music by
GEORGE HARRISON

© 1969 HARRISONGS LTD.

91

HELP!

Words and Music by
JOHN LENNON and PAUL McCARTNEY

Moderately, with a driving beat

Help!   I need some-bod - y,
Help!   Not just an-y-bod-y, Help!   You know I
need some-one, ___   Help! ___

1.,3. When I ___ was young-er, so ___ much
2. And now ___ my life has changed ___ in,

young - er than to - day, _____
oh, so man - y ways, _____

I nev-er need-ed an-y-bod - y's
My in-de-pen-dence seems to

Help in an-y way. ___ But now these
van-ish in the haze. ___ But ev-'ry

© 1965 NORTHERN SONGS LTD.
Copyright Renewed
All Rights Controlled and Administered by EMI BLACKWOOD MUSIC INC.
under license from ATV MUSIC CORP. (MACLEN MUSIC)

HERE, THERE AND EVERYWHERE

Words and Music by
JOHN LENNON and PAUL McCARTNEY

Ad lib.

To lead a bet-ter life _ I need my love to be here. _

Moderately slow

Here, mak-ing each day _ of the year,

chang-ing my life _ with a wave _ of her hand. _

No-bod-y can _ de-ny _ that there's some - thing there. _

There, run-ning my hands _ through her hair, _

both of us think - ing how good _ it can be. _

Some-one is speak - ing, but she does-n't know _ he's there. _

© 1966 NORTHERN SONGS LTD.
Copyright Renewed
All Rights Controlled and Administered by EMI BLACKWOOD MUSIC INC.
under license from ATV MUSIC CORP. (MACLEN MUSIC)

HEY JUDE

Words and Music by
JOHN LENNON and PAUL McCARTNEY

© 1968 NORTHERN SONGS LTD.
All Rights Controlled and Administered by EMI BLACKWOOD MUSIC INC.
under license from ATV MUSIC CORP. (MACLEN MUSIC)

I AM THE WALRUS

Words and Music by
JOHN LENNON and PAUL McCARTNEY

Slow 4

I am he as you are he as you are me and we are all to-geth-
Ex-pert tex-pert chok-ing smok-ers, don't you think the jok-er laughs at you?

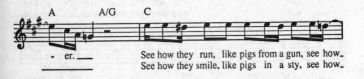

- er. See how they run, like pigs from a gun, see how
See how they smile, like pigs in a sty, see how

they fly I'm cry - ing.
they hide. I'm cry - ing.

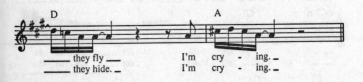

Sit-ting on a corn - flake wait - ing for the van to come
Yel-low mat-ter cus - tard drip-ping from a dead dog's eye
Sem-o - li - na pil - chards climb-ing up the Eif - fel Tow-

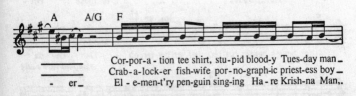

Cor-por-a - tion tee shirt, stu-pid blood-y Tues-day man
Crab-a-lock-er fish-wife por-no-graph-ic priest-ess boy
- er El - e-men-t'ry pen-guin sing-ing Ha - re Krish-na Man,

© 1967 COMET MUSIC CORP.
All Rights Controlled and Administered by EMI APRIL MUSIC INC.
under license from WELBECK MUSIC CORP. (COMET)

— you been a naught - y boy _ you let your face grow long. _
— you been a naught - y girl, _ you let your knick - ers down. _
— you should have seen them kick - ing Ed - gar Al - lan Poe. _

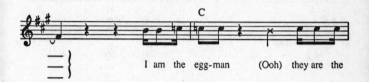

I am the egg-man (Ooh) they are the

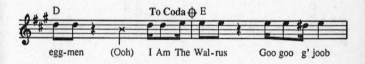

egg-men (Ooh) I Am The Wal-rus Goo goo g' joob

To Coda ⊕ **E**

Mis-ter cit-y p'lice-man sit-ting pret-ty lit-tle p'lice-men in a row.

1. | A | A/G | C | D | E

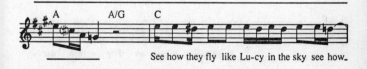

See how they fly like Lu-cy in the sky see how. _

A | A/G | C

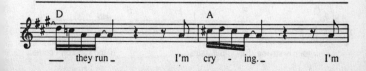

_ they run _ I'm cry - ing. _ I'm

D | A

100

cry - ing   I'm

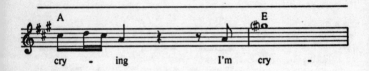

cry - ing   I'm   cry -

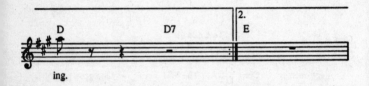

ing.

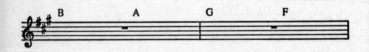

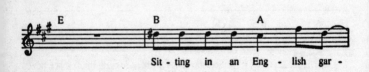

Sit - ting   in   an   Eng - lish   gar -

- den wait-ing for   the sun,___   if the sun don't come,___

B7

— you get a tan from stand - ing in the Eng - lish rain..

C

I am the egg-man   They are the

D   **D7**   **E**

egg-men   I Am The Wal-rus,   Goo goo g' joob g' goo.

D   D.C. al Coda   **CODA** ⊕   **E**

— goo g' joob.   Wal-rus   Goo goo g' joob g' goo -

D   **C**

— goo g' joob   Goo goo g' goo g' goo - goo g' joob

Bsus   **A**

joob   (Instrumental)

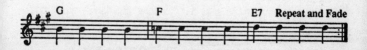

G   **F**   **E7**   **Repeat and Fade**

I DON'T WANT TO SPOIL THE PARTY

Words and Music by
JOHN LENNON and PAUL McCARTNEY

I Don't Want To Spoil The Par - ty, so I'll
had a drink or two and I don't

go. _____ I would hate my dis - ap -
care. _____ There's no fun in what I

point - ment to show. _____ There's
do if she's not there. _____ I

noth - ing for me here, so I will dis - ap - pear. .
won - der what went wrong. I've wait - ed far too long. .

___ If she turns up while i'm gone please let me
___ I think I'll take a walk and look for

know. ___ I've
her. ___

Though to - night she's made me sad, .

___ I still love her. If I

© 1964 NORTHERN SONGS LTD.
Copyright Renewed
All Rights Controlled and Administered by EMI BLACKWOOD MUSIC INC.
under license from ATV MUSIC CORP. (MACLEN MUSIC)

I FEEL FINE

Words and Music by
JOHN LENNON and PAUL McCARTNEY

Bright Rock

(Instrumental)

§ G7

Ba - by's good to me, ___ you know, ___ she's
Ba - by says she's mine, ___ you know, ___ she
Ba - by says she's mine, ___ you know, ___ she

hap - py as can be, ___ you know, ___ she
tells me all the time, ___ you know, ___ she
tells me all the time, ___ you know, ___ she

D

said so. I'm in love ___ with
said so. I'm in love ___ with
said so. I'm in love ___ with

C   Bb/C   1. G7   2.,3. G7

her and I ___ Feel ___ Fine. ___
her and I ___ Feel ___ Fine. ___
her and I ___ Feel ___ Fine. ___

© 1964 NORTHERN SONGS LTD.
Copyright Renewed
All Rights Controlled and Administered by EMI BLACKWOOD MUSIC INC.
under license from ATV MUSIC CORP. (MACLEN MUSIC)

G   **Bm**   **C**

I'm so glad that she's my lit-tle girl..

D   **G**   **Bm**   **C**

She's so glad she's tell-ing all_ the world.

D   **G7**

that her ba-by buys her things,_ you know,_ he

D

buys her dia-mond rings_ you know,_ she said so.

To Coda ⊕

C

She's in love_ with me and I _ Feel_ Fine..

G7   **D.S. al Coda**   **CODA** ⊕ **G7**

D   **C**   **G7 N.C.**

She's in love_ with me and I _ Feel_ Fine. _

Repeat and Fade

(Instrumental)

I SAW HER STANDING THERE

Words and Music by
JOHN LENNON and PAUL McCARTNEY

Well, she was just _____ sev-en-teen,
looked at me, _____

_____ and you know what I mean, And the
and I, I could see _____ That be-

way she looked _ was way be-yond com-pare. _____
fore too long _ I'd fall in love with her. _____

So how could I dance _ with an-oth-
She would-n't dance _ with an-oth-

-er, _ woo, — } When I Saw Her
-er, _ woo, — }

Stand-ing There. _

Well, she_

© 1963 NORTHERN SONGS LTD.
Copyright Renewed
All Rights for the United States of America, its territories and possessions and Canada
assigned to and controlled by GIL MUSIC CORP., 1650 Broadway, New York, NY

Well my heart went boom — when I

crossed that room, — and I held her hand —

— in mi - een, ——— een, ———

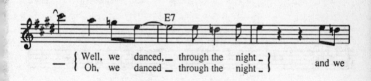

— { Well, we danced, — through the night — }
{ Oh, we danced — through the night — } and we

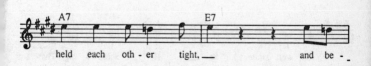

held each oth - er tight, — and be - -

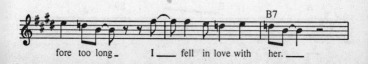

fore too long — I — fell in love with her. —

108

Now I'll nev-er dance_ with an-oth-

-er,_ Oh,_ since I Saw Her

Stand - ing There._ Well my

CODA

Oh, since I Saw_

_ Her Stand - ing There._

Yeah, well since I Saw_ Her Stand - ing There._

(Instrumental)

I SHOULD HAVE KNOWN BETTER

Words and Music by
JOHN LENNON and PAUL McCARTNEY

Moderately

(Instrumental)

I _____ Should Have Known __
I _____ nev - er re - al -

Bet - ter with a girl like you, __ that I would
ized __ what a kiss could be, __ this could

love ev - 'ry-thing that you do; __ And I do, __
on - ly __ hap - pen to me; __ Can't you see?_

1.
_ hey, hey, hey, __ and I do. __

© 1964 NORTHERN SONGS LTD.
Copyright Renewed
All Rights Controlled and Administered by EMI BLACKWOOD MUSIC INC.
under license from ATV MUSIC CORP. (MACLEN MUSIC)

Wo — wo —

Can't you see? — That when I

tell you that I love — you, — oh! —

You're gon - na say — you love me too —

— hoo hoo hoo — hoo, oh. —

And when I ask you to be mi -

- ah - ha - hine — you're gon - na say —

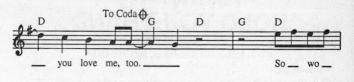

you love me, too. _____ So _ wo _

I _____ should have re - al -

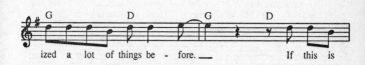

ized a lot of things be - fore. _ If this is

love, you got - ta give me more; _ give me more,

_ hey, hey, hey, _ give me more.

_ So _ wo _

_____ You love me, too. _

I WANT TO HOLD YOUR HAND

Words and Music by
JOHN LENNON and PAUL McCARTNEY

Moderately

Oh yeah, I'll ___ tell you some-thing
please ___ say to me

I think you'll un-der-stand. When I ___ say that
you'll let me be your man, And please ___ say to

some-thing,
me

I Want To Hold Your Hand, ___
you'll let me hold your hand, ___

I Want To Hold Your Hand, ___
Now let me hold your hand, ___

1.
I Want To Hold Your Hand. Oh, ___

2.
I Want To Hold Your Hand.

And when I touch you I feel

hap-py ___ in-side. ___ It's such a

© Copyright 1963 NORTHERN SONGS
Copyright Renewed
All Rights Controlled and Administered by MCA MUSIC PUBLISHING,
A Division of MCA INC. under license from NORTHERN SONGS

I WILL

Words and Music by
JOHN LENNON and PAUL McCARTNEY

Who knows _ how long _ I've loved _ you? _ You know _
_ I ev- er saw _ you, _ I did-

I love _ you still. _ Will I wait
-n't catch _ your name, _ But it nev-

_ a lone- ly life- time? If you want _
-er real- ly mat- tered, I will al-

1.
_ me to, _ I Will. _ For if _
-ways feel _ the same. _

2.
Love you for- ev- er and _ for- ev- er,

Love you with all _ my heart, _

Love you when- ev- er we're _ to- geth- er,

© 1968 NORTHERN SONGS LTD.
All Rights Controlled and Administered by EMI BLACKWOOD MUSIC INC.
under license from ATV MUSIC CORP. (MACLEN MUSIC)

I'LL FOLLOW THE SUN

Words and Music by
JOHN LENNON and PAUL McCARTNEY

One day __ you'll look __
Some day __ you'll know __
(Instrumental ad lib.)

to see I've gone, __ For to-
I was the one, __ But to-
Yeah, to-

mor-row may rain, __ so __ I'll Fol-low The
mor-row may rain, __ so __ I'll Fol-low The
mor-row may rain, __ so __ I'll Fol-low The

1.
Sun.

2.

Sun. }
Sun. }

And now the time has come, __ And

© 1964 NORTHERN SONGS LTD.
Copyright Renewed
All Rights Controlled and Administered by EMI BLACKWOOD MUSIC INC.
under license from ATV MUSIC CORP. (MACLEN MUSIC)

I'M A LOSER

Words and Music by
JOHN LENNON and PAUL McCARTNEY

Ad lib.

Am7 — I'm A Los - er, I'm a

Am7 — los - er, And I'm

Am7 — not what I ap - pear to be. — F — D7

G — Of all the love I have won — D
Al - though I laugh and I act
What have I done to de - serve

F — or have lost There is one love — G
like a clown — Be - neath this mask
such a fate — I re - a - lize

D — I should nev - er have crossed. — F — G
I am wear - ing a frown.
I have left it too late.

© 1964 NORTHERN SONGS LTD.
Copyright Renewed
All Rights Controlled and Administered by EMI BLACKWOOD MUSIC INC.
under license from ATV MUSIC CORP. (MACLEN MUSIC)

I'M HAPPY JUST TO DANCE WITH YOU

Words and Music by
JOHN LENNON and PAUL McCARTNEY

Be-fore this dance is through,_ I think I'll love you too,_ I'm so
hap - py when you dance with me. I don't

want to kiss or hold your hand,_ If it's
need to hug or hold you tight,_ I just

fun - ny try and un - der - stand._ There is
wan - na dance with you all night._ In this

real - ly noth-ing else I'd rath - er do,_ } 'Cause I'm
world there's noth-ing I would rath - er do,_

© 1964 NORTHERN SONGS LTD.
Copyright Renewed
All Rights Controlled and Administered by EMI BLACKWOOD MUSIC INC.
under license from ATV MUSIC CORP. (MACLEN MUSIC)

Hap - py Just To Dance With You. I don't

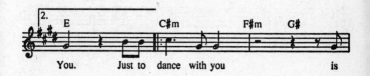

You. Just to dance with you is

ev - 'ry - thing I need. Be - fore this

dance is through, I think I'll love you too, I'm so

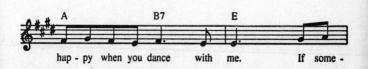

hap - py when you dance with me. If some -

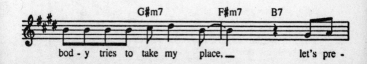

bod - y tries to take my place, let's pre -

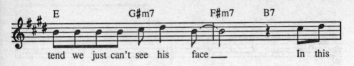

tend we just can't see his face ___ In this

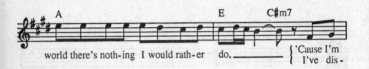

world there's noth-ing I would rath-er do, ___ { 'Cause I'm
  { I've dis-

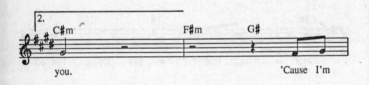

1. E

Hap - py Just To Dance With You. Just to
cov-ered I'm in love with

2. C#m

you. 'Cause I'm

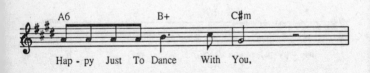

Hap - py Just To Dance With You,

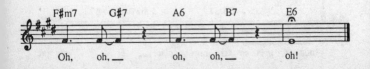

Oh, oh, ___ oh, oh, ___ oh!

I'M LOOKING THROUGH YOU

Words and Music by
JOHN LENNON and PAUL McCARTNEY

© 1965 NORTHERN SONGS LTD.
Copyright Renewed
All Rights Controlled and Administered by EMI BLACKWOOD MUSIC INC.
under license from ATV MUSIC CORP. (MACLEN MUSIC)

Why, tell me why ___ did you ___ not

treat me right? ___ Love has a nas-

- ty hab-it of dis-ap-pear - ing o-ver night. ___

{ You're think-ing of me the same ___ old ___
  I'm Look-ing Through You, where did ___ you go?. ___

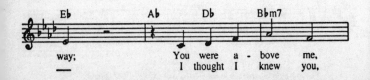

way; You were a - bove me,
___ I thought I knew you,

I'VE JUST SEEN A FACE

Words and Music by
JOHN LENNON and PAUL McCARTNEY

Brightly, in 2

I've Just Seen A Face I can't for - get the time_ or
place where we just met. She's just the girl_ for me and I_
_ want all the world to see_ we've met.

Mm mm mm mm _ mm. _

To Coda

Had it been_ an - oth - er day_ I might have looked the
I have nev - er known the like_ of this I've been a -
Instrumental

oth - er way_ and I'd have nev - er been_ a - ware._ But
lone and I_ have missed things and kept out_ of sight._ For

as it is I'll dream of her_ to - night, _
oth - er girls were nev - er quite_ like this, _

© 1965 NORTHERN SONGS LTD.
Copyright Renewed
All Rights Controlled and Administered by EMI BLACKWOOD MUSIC INC.
under license from ATV MUSIC CORP. (MACLEN MUSIC)

IF I FELL

Words and Music by
JOHN LENNON and PAUL McCARTNEY

© 1964 NORTHERN SONGS LTD.
Copyright Renewed
All Rights Controlled and Administered by EMI BLACKWOOD MUSIC INC.
under license from ATV MUSIC CORP. (MACLEN MUSIC)

IN MY LIFE

Words and Music by
JOHN LENNON and PAUL McCARTNEY

Moderately

(Instrumental)

There are plac- es I'll re-
But of all these friends and

mem- ber all my life, _____ though
lov- ers there is no _____ one com-

some have changed._ Some for- ev- er, not for
pares with you. _____ And these mem- 'ries lose their

bet- ter; Some have gone _____ and
mean- ing when I think of _ love as

some re- main._ All these plac- es _____ had _ their
some- thing new._ Tho' I know_ I'll _ nev- er lose af-

mo- ments with lov- ers and friends _ I
fec- tion for peo- ple and things _ that

© 1965 NORTHERN SONGS LTD.
Copyright Renewed
All Rights Controlled and Administered by EMI BLACKWOOD MUSIC INC.
under license from ATV MUSIC CORP. (MACLEN MUSIC)

still can re-call. _ Some are dead _ and _ some _ are _
went _ be-fore, _ I know I'll of-ten stop and think a-

liv – ing, _ In My _____ Life I've
bout them, _ In My _____ Life I

To Coda

loved them all. _ *(Instrumental)*
love you more. _

1.

2. **D.S. al Coda**

Tho' I

CODA

(Instrumental) In

My _____ Life I love you

more.
(Instrumental)

IT'S ONLY LOVE

Words and Music by
JOHN LENNON and PAUL McCARTNEY

© 1965 NORTHERN SONGS LTD.
Copyright Renewed
All Rights Controlled and Administered by EMI BLACKWOOD MUSIC INC.
under license from ATV MUSIC CORP. (MACLEN MUSIC)

I'M ONLY SLEEPING

Words and Music by
JOHN LENNON and PAUL McCARTNEY

© 1966 NORTHERN SONGS LTD.
All Rights Controlled and Administered by EMI BLACKWOOD MUSIC INC.
under license from ATV MUSIC CORP. (MACLEN MUSIC)

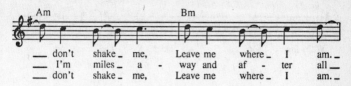

Am / **Bm**

_ don't shake _ me, Leave me where _ I am. _
_ I'm miles _ a - way and af - ter all _
_ don't shake _ me, Leave me where _ I am. _

Am **Gmaj7** **To Coda ⊕**

_ } I'm On - ly Sleep - ing. ____

Am7 **Em**

Dm7 **E7**

Keep-ing an eye _ on the world _ go-ing by _ my

Am **Am7** **Fmaj7**

win - dow, Tak - ing my time ____

Em **Am**

ly - ing there and star - ing at the ceil - ing,

136

Wait-ing for ___ a sleep-y feel - ing.

Please don't wake ___ me, no, ___ don't shake ___ me,

Leave me where ___ I am. ___ I'm On - ly

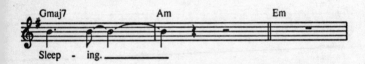

Sleep - ing. ___

Keep - ing an eye ___ on the world ___

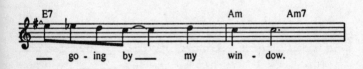

___ go - ing by ___ my win - dow.

Tak-ing my time. ___

JULIA

Words and Music by
JOHN LENNON and PAUL McCARTNEY

© 1968 NORTHERN SONGS LTD.
All Rights Controlled and Administered by EMI BLACKWOOD MUSIC INC.
under license from ATV MUSIC CORP. (MACLEN MUSIC)

LADY MADONNA

Words and Music by
JOHN LENNON and PAUL McCARTNEY

Brightly, with a beat

(Instrumental)

Lady Madonna, children at your feet,
Lady Madonna, baby at your breast,
Lady Madonna, lying on the bed,
Lady Madonna, children at your feet,

Wonder how you manage to make
Wonders how you manage to feed
Listen to the music playing
Wonder how you manage to make

To Coda

ends meet. Who finds the mon-
the rest. (Instrumental ad lib.)
in your head. (Instrumental ad lib.)
ends meet.

-ey when you pay the rent,

© 1968 NORTHERN SONGS LTD.
All Rights Controlled and Administered by EMI BLACKWOOD MUSIC INC.
under license from ATV MUSIC CORP. (MACLEN MUSIC)

Did you think that mon-ey was heav-en sent?

Fri-day night ar-rives with-out a suit-case,
3. Tues-day af-ter-noon is nev-er end-ing,

Sun-day morn-ing creep-ing like a
Wednes-day morn-ing pa-pers did-n't

nun, Mon-day's child has learned to tie his
come, Thurs-day night your stock-ings need-ed

boot-lace, }
mend-ing. }   See

how they run!

CODA

(Instrumental)

THE LONG AND WINDING ROAD

Words and Music by
JOHN LENNON and PAUL McCARTNEY

© 1970 NORTHERN SONGS LTD.
All Rights Controlled and Administered by EMI BLACKWOOD MUSIC INC.
under license from ATV MUSIC CORP. (MACLEN MUSIC)

still they lead me back to The Long Wind-ing Road.

You left me stand - ing here

a long, long time a - go.

Don't {leave / keep} me wait - ing here.

To Coda

Lead me to your door.

(Instrumental)

D.S. al Coda

But

CODA

door. Yeah, yeah, yeah, yeah.

LOVE ME DO

Words and Music by
JOHN LENNON and PAUL McCARTNEY

© 1962, 1963 (Renewed 1990, 1991) MPL COMMUNICATIONS LTD., JULIAN LENNON,
SEAN ONO LENNON and YOKO ONO LENNON
All Rights for the U.S. Controlled and Administered by BEECHWOOD MUSIC CORP.,
JULIAN LENNON, SEAN ONO LENNON and YOKO ONO LENNON
All Rights for Canada Controlled and Administered by BEECHWOOD MUSIC CORP.

LOVELY RITA

Words and Music by
JOHN LENNON and PAUL McCARTNEY

© 1967 NORTHERN SONGS LTD.
All Rights Controlled and Administered by EMI BLACKWOOD MUSIC INC.
under license from ATV MUSIC CORP. (MACLEN MUSIC)

and the bag a - cross her shoul - der
took her home, I near - ly made _ it,

made her look a lit-tle like a mil-i-t'ry man._
sit - ting on the so-fa with a sis-ter or two._ Oh, ___

Love-ly Ri-ta, me-ter maid, _ may I en-quire dis-creet - ly,
Love-ly Ri-ta, me-ter maid, _ where would I be with-out you?

"When are you free to take some tea with me?"
Give us a wink and make me think of

Ah. ___ Ri-ta *(Instrumental)*

you.
Love-ly Ri-ta, me-ter maid, _

Love - ly Ri - ta, _ me-ter maid. _ Love - ly Ri - ta,

me-ter maid, _ Love - ly Ri - ta, _ me-ter maid. _

LUCY IN THE SKY
WITH DIAMONDS

Words and Music by
JOHN LENNON and PAUL McCARTNEY

(Instrumental)

Pic - ture your - self in a boat on a riv - er with
Fol - low her down to a bridge by a foun - tain where
Pic - ture your - self on a train in a sta - tion with

tan - ger - ine trees and mar - ma - lade skies.
rock - ing horse peo - ple eat marsh - mal - low pies.
plas - ti - cine por - ters with look - ing glass ties.

Some - bod - y calls you, you an - swer quite
Ev - 'ry - one smiles as you drift past the
Sud - den - ly some - one is there at the

slow - ly, a girl with ka - lei - do - scope
flow - ers that grow so in - cred - i - bly
turn - stile, the girl with ka - lei - do - scope

To Coda ⊕

eyes. _____
high. _____

Cel - lo - phane
News - pa - per

© 1967 NORTHERN SONGS LTD.
All Rights Controlled and Administered by EMI BLACKWOOD MUSIC INC.
under license from ATV MUSIC CORP. (MACLEN MUSIC)

LET IT BE

Words and Music by
JOHN LENNON and PAUL McCARTNEY

© 1970 NORTHERN SONGS LTD.
All Rights Controlled and Administered by EMI BLACKWOOD MUSIC INC.
under license from ATV MUSIC CORP. (MACLEN MUSIC)

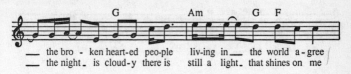

the bro - ken heart-ed peo-ple liv-ing in ___ the world a - gree
the night _ is cloud-y there is still a light _ that shines on me

There will be an an - swer, Let It Be. ___ For
Sine un - til to-mor - row. Let It Be. ___ I

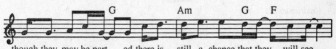

though they may be part - ed there is still a chance that they ___ will see ___
wake up to the sound _ of mu-sic Moth-er Mar - y comes. to me ___

There will be an an - swer, Let It Be. ___ }
Speak-ing words of wis - dom, Let It Be. ___ } Let It Be, _

___ Let It Be, ___ Let It Be, ___ Let It Be, ___

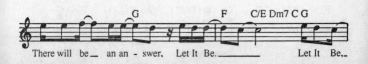

There will be ___ an an - swer, Let It Be. ___ Let It Be, _

Let It Be,__ Let It Be,__ Let It Be,_

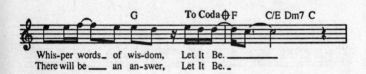

Whis-per words__ of wis-dom, Let It Be._____
There will be ___ an an-swer, Let It Be. _

(Instrumental)

D.S. al Coda

CODA

Let It Be,__ Let It Be,__ Let It Be,_

__ Let It Be.__ Whis-per words__ of wis - dom, Let It Be._

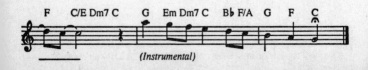

(Instrumental)

MAXWELL'S SILVER HAMMER

Words and Music by
JOHN LENNON and PAUL McCARTNEY

Moderately

D7
Joan was quiz-zi-cal, stud-ied pat-a-phys-i-cal
Back in school a-gain, Max-well plays the fool a-gain,
P. C. Thir-ty-one said, "We've caught a dir-ty one,"

Em
sci-ence in the home
teach-er gets an-noyed.
Max-well stand a-lone

A7
Late nights all a-lone with a test-tube,
Wish-ing to a-void an un-pleas-ant
Paint-ing tes-ti-mo-ni-al pic-tures,

D **A** **D**
oh, oh, oh, oh. Max-well Ed-i-son,
sce-e-e-ene, She tells Max to stay
oh, oh, oh, oh. Rose and Val-er-ie

B7 **Em**
ma-jor-ing in med-i-cine, calls her on the phone:
when the class has gone a-way. So he waits be-hind
scream-ing from the gal-ler-y say he must go free.

© 1969 NORTHERN SONGS LTD.
All Rights Controlled and Administered by EMI BLACKWOOD MUSIC INC.
under license from ATV MUSIC CORP. (MACLEN MUSIC)

155

Sil - ver Ham - mer made sure that she was dead.
Sil - ver Ham - mer made
Sil - ver Ham - mer made

(Instrumental)

sure that she was dead.

(Instrumental)

Sil - ver ham - mer.

MAGICAL MYSTERY TOUR

Words and Music by
JOHN LENNON and PAUL McCARTNEY

© 1967 COMET MUSIC CORP.
All Rights Controlled and Administered by EMI APRIL MUSIC INC.
under license from WELBECK MUSIC CORP. (COMET)

MARTHA MY DEAR

Words and Music by
JOHN LENNON and PAUL McCARTNEY

(Instrumental)

Mar-tha, My Dear, though I spend my days in con-ver-sa-tion, please, re-mem-ber me. Mar-tha, my love,

© 1968 NORTHERN SONGS LTD.
All Rights Controlled and Administered by EMI BLACKWOOD MUSIC INC.
under license from ATV MUSIC CORP. (MACLEN MUSIC)

Bb7   Ab   Bb7

don't for-get _ me._____

Ab   Bb7

Mar - tha My _ Dear._____

Dm7   Gm9

Hold   your   head___   up,   you   sil - ly   girl: __
Hold   your   hand___   out,   you   sil - ly   girl; __

F6

Look   what you've   done._____
See   what you've   done._____

Gm/C

When __ you   find ___ your-self __ in the
When __ you   find ___ your-self __ in the

C7   Gm/C

thick   of   it,   help   your - self ___   to   a
thick   of   it,   help   your - self ___   to   a

C7   A   Dm7

bit   of   what   is   all   a - round ___   you,
bit   of   what   is   all   a - round ___   you,

Gm7   To Coda ⊕

sil - ly   girl. __   Take   a
sil - ly   girl. __

160

Mar - tha ___ My Dear, ___ you have al -

- ways been my in-spi - ra - tion; Please ___

___ be good to me ___ Mar - tha, my ___ love ___

___ don't for-get ___ me, ___

Mar - tha, My ___ Dear. ___ *(Instrumental)*

MICHELLE

Words and Music by
JOHN LENNON and PAUL McCARTNEY

© 1965 NORTHERN SONGS LTD.
Copyright Renewed
All Rights Controlled and Administered by EMI BLACKWOOD MUSIC INC.
under license from ATV MUSIC CORP. (MACLEN MUSIC)

(Instrumental)

want you, I want you, I want ___ you, I think you know by now, I'll get to you some - how. ___ Un - til I do, I'm tell - ing you, so you'll un - der - stand; Mi - chelle, ma belle, sont des mots qui vont tres bien en-semble, tres bien en - semble. And I will say the on - ly words _ I know that you'll un - der - stand, my Mi - chelle. (Instrumental)

Repeat and Fade

MOTHER NATURE'S SON

Words and Music by
JOHN LENNON and PAUL McCARTNEY

Born a poor young
Sit be-side a
Find me in a

coun-try boy, Moth-er Na-ture's Son.
moun-tain stream, see her wa-ters rise.
field of grass, Moth-er Na-ture's Son.

All day long I'm sit-ting, sing-ing songs for ev-'ry-one.
Lis-ten to the pret-ty sound of mus-ic as she flies.
Sway-ing dai-sies sing a laz-y song be-neath the sun.
Mm Ah - wa-wa

(Instrumental)

Du du

© 1968 NORTHERN SONGS LTD.
All Rights Controlled and Administered by EMI BLACKWOOD MUSIC INC.
under license from ATV MUSIC CORP. (MACLEN MUSIC)

NOWHERE MAN

Words and Music by
JOHN LENNON and PAUL McCARTNEY

Moderately

He's a real No-where Man, sit-ting in his no-where land, mak-ing all his no-where plans for no-bod-y.

Does-n't have a point of view, knows not where he's go-ing to, is-n't he a bit like you and me?

He's as blind as he can be, just sees what he wants to see, No-where Man, can you see me at all?

No-where Man, please lis-ten: you don't know what you're miss-ing. No-where Man, the

No-where Man, don't wor-ry, take your time, don't hur-ry. Leave it all till

please lis-ten: you don't know what you're miss-ing. No-where Man, the

© 1965 NORTHERN SONGS LTD.
Copyright Renewed
All Rights Controlled and Administered by EMI BLACKWOOD MUSIC INC.
under license from ATV MUSIC CORP. (MACLEN MUSIC)

F#m

world _____ is at your com-mand,
some - bod - y else lends you a hand.
world _____ is at your com-mand.

B

E B A

(Instrumental ad lib.)

Does-n't have _ a point of view, _ knows not where he's
He's a real _ No - where Man, _ sit - ting in his

E To Coda ⊕ A Am

go - ing to _ }
no-where land. _ }
is-n't he _ a bit _ like you _ and

1. E

me? _____

2. E

me? _____

D.S. al Coda

No-where Man, _

CODA ⊕

A Am

Mak-ing all _ his no - where plans for

E A

no - bod - y. _ Mak-ing all _ his

Am E

no - where plans for no - bod - y.

NORWEGIAN WOOD
(THIS BIRD HAS FLOWN)

Words and Music by
JOHN LENNON and PAUL McCARTNEY

© 1965 NORTHERN SONGS LTD.
Copyright Renewed
All Rights Controlled and Administered by EMI BLACKWOOD MUSIC INC.
under license from ATV MUSIC CORP. (MACLEN MUSIC)

OB-LA-DI, OB-LA-DA

Words and Music by
JOHN LENNON and PAUL McCARTNEY

Des-mond has his bar-row in the mar-ket place;— Mol-
Des-mond takes a trol-ley to the jewel-er's store,— buys—

-ly is the sing-er in a band. Des-
— a twen-ty car-at gol-den ring. Takes—

-mond says to Mol-ly, "Girl, I like your face,"
— it back to Mol-ly wait-ing at the door—

— and Mol-ly says this as she takes him by the hand:—
— and as he gives it to her she be-gins to sing:—

— Ob-la-di — Ob-la-da — life goes on —

— bra — la — la how the life goes on.—

— Ob-la-di — Ob-la-da — life goes on —

© 1968 NORTHERN SONGS LTD.
All Rights Controlled and Administered by EMI BLACKWOOD MUSIC INC.
under license from ATV MUSIC CORP. (MACLEN MUSIC)

OH! DARLING

Words and Music by
JOHN LENNON and PAUL McCARTNEY

© 1969 NORTHERN SONGS LTD.
All Rights Controlled and Administered by EMI BLACKWOOD MUSIC, INC.
under license from ATV MUSIC CORP. (MACLEN MUSIC)

PAPERBACK WRITER

Words and Music by
JOHN LENNON and PAUL McCARTNEY

Bright Rock

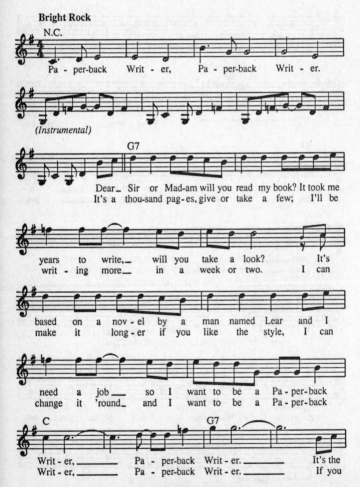

Pa - per-back Writ - er, Pa - per-back Writ - er.

(Instrumental)

Dear_ Sir or Mad-am will you read my book? It took me
It's a thou-sand pag-es, give or take a few; I'll be

years to write,_ will you take a look? It's
writ-ing more_ in a week or two. I can

based on a nov-el by a man named Lear and I
make it long-er if you like the style, I can

need a job_ so I want to be a Pa-per-back
change it 'round_ and I want to be a Pa-per-back

Writ-er,_ Pa - per-back Writ-er._ It's the
Writ-er,_ Pa - per-back Writ-er._ If you

© 1966 NORTHERN SONGS LTD.
All Rights Controlled and Administered by EMI BLACKWOOD MUSIC INC.
under license from ATV MUSIC CORP. (MACLEN MUSIC)

dirt - y sto - ry of a dirt - y man, __ and his
real - ly like it you can have the rights, __ it could

cling-ing wife __ does-n't un-der-stand. His son is work - ing for the
make a mil-lion for you o-ver-night. If you must re - turn __ it you can

Dai - ly Mail; __ it's a stead - y job __ but he
send it here, __ but I need a break __ and I

wants to be a Pa-per-back Writ - er, _____ Pa - per-back
want to be a Pa-per-back Writ - er, _____ Pa - per-back

Writ - er. _____
Writ - er. _____ Pa-per-back Writ - er,

Pa - per-back Writ - er. *(Instrumental)*

Pa - per-back Writ - er. _____

Repeat and Fade

PLEASE PLEASE ME

Words and Music by
JOHN LENNON and PAUL McCARTNEY

Moderately, with a beat

1.,3. Last night I said these words to my _____ girl,
2. You don't need me to show the way _____ love,

I know {you / I} nev - er e - ven try, _____ girl.
why do I al - ways have to say, _____ love.

Come on (Come on) _____ Come on (Come on) _____ Come on (Come on) _____ Come on, (Come on) _____ Please,

Please, Please me, wo yeah, like I please you.

Copyright © 1962 Dick James Music Ltd., Julian Lennon, Sean Ono Lennon and Yoko Ono Lennon
Copyright Renewed
All Rights for Dick James Music Ltd. in the United States Administered by
Songs Of PolyGram International, Inc.

I don't want to sound com-plain-ing

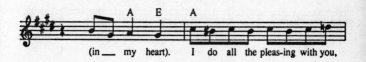

but you know there's al-ways rain in my _____ heart.

(in _____ my heart). I do all the pleas-ing with you,

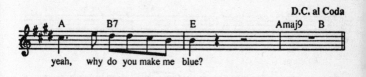

it's so hard to rea-son with you, wo

D.C. al Coda

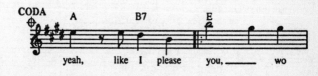

yeah, why do you make me blue?

CODA

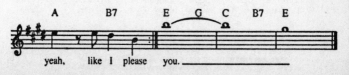

yeah, like I please you, _____ wo

yeah, like I please you. _____

P.S. I LOVE YOU

Words and Music by
JOHN LENNON and PAUL McCARTNEY

Moderate Rock

As I write this let-ter, send my love to you. Re-mem-ber that I'll al-ways be in love with you. Trea-sure these few words till we're to-geth-er, Keep all my love for-ev-er, P. S. I Love You, you, you, you.

1.,3. I'll be com-ing home a-gain to you love and
2. Treas-ure these few words till we're to-geth-er, keep

© 1962, 1963 (Renewed 1990, 1991) MPL COMMUNICATIONS LTD.,
JULIAN LENNON, SEAN ONO LENNON and YOKO ONO LENNON
All Rights for the U.S. Controlled and Administered by BEECHWOOD MUSIC CORP.,
JULIAN LENNON, SEAN ONO LENNON and YOKO ONO LENNON
All Rights for Canada Controlled and Administered by BEECHWOOD MUSIC CORP.

PENNY LANE

Words and Music by
JOHN LENNON and PAUL McCARTNEY

Medium Swing tempo

Pen-ny Lane:___ there is a bar - ber show-ing
shel - ter in the mid - dle of the

pho-to-graphs___ of ev'-ry head___ he's had the plea-sure to know.
round-a-bout,___ the pret-ty nurse___ is sell-ing pop-pies from a tray.

And all the peo - ple that come and go___
And tho' she feels as if she's in a play___

stop and say___ hel - lo.
she is an - y-way.

On the Pen-ny

cor - ner is a bank - er with a mo-tor-car;___ The lit - tle chil-
Lane: the bar - ber shaves an - oth - er cus-tom-er,___ We see the bank-

- dren laugh at him be - hind his back. And the
- er sit - ting wait-ing for a trim. And then the

bank - er nev - er wears a mac___ in the pour - ing rain,
fire - man rush - es in___ from the pour - ing rain,

© 1967 NORTHERN SONGS LTD.
All Rights Controlled and Administered by EMI BLACKWOOD MUSIC INC.
under license from ATV MUSIC CORP. (MACLEN MUSIC)

RAIN

Words and Music by
JOHN LENNON and PAUL McCARTNEY

© 1966 NORTHERN SONGS LTD.
All Rights Controlled and Administered by EMI BLACKWOOD MUSIC INC.
under license from ATV MUSIC CORP. (MACLEN MUSIC)

REVOLUTION

Words and Music by
JOHN LENNON and PAUL McCARTNEY

© 1968 NORTHERN SONGS LTD.
All Rights Controlled and Administered by EMI BLACKWOOD MUSIC INC.
under license from ATV MUSIC CORP. (MACLEN MUSIC)

But when you talk a-bout de-struc-tion,_____
But if you want money for people with minds that hate,_____
But if you go carry-ing pictures of Chair-man Mao,_____

Don't you know that you can count me out._
All I can tell you is, "Brother you have to wait."_
You ain't going to make it with any-one an-y-how._

Don't you know it's gon-na be_____ al - right,_

al - right, _____ al - right._

(Instrumental)

1.,2.
You
You

3.
Al - right,_ al - right, _ al - right._

_ al - right,_ al - right, _ al - right,_

_ al - right,_ al - right. (Instrumental)

ROCKY RACCOON

Words and Music by
JOHN LENNON and PAUL McCARTNEY

Moderately, in two (♩=1 beat)

(Spoken:) Now somewhere in the Black Mountain Hills of Dakota there lived a eye. Rocky didn't like that. He said: "I'm going to get that boy."

young boy named Rocky Raccoon. And one day his woman ran off with another
So one day he walked into town and booked himself a

guy, hit young Rocky in the
room in the local saloon. Rock - y Rac - coon____ checked
she and her man____ who

in - to his room____ on - ly to find____ Gid-eon's Bi -
called him-self Dan____ were in the next room____ at the hoe -

- ble.____ Rock - y had come e -
- down.____ Rock - y burst in____ and

quipped with a gun____ to shoot off the legs____ of his ri -
grin - ning a grin,____ He said, "Dan-ny boy, this____ is a show -

- val.____ His ri - val it seems____ had
- down."____ But Dan - iel was hot,____ he

© 1968, 1969 NORTHERN SONGS LTD.
All Rights Controlled and Administered by EMI BLACKWOOD MUSIC INC.
under license from ATV MUSIC CORP. (MACLEN MUSIC)

D7sus | D7 | G7

bro-ken his dreams_ by steal-ing the girl__ of his fan-
drew first and shot__ and Rock-y col-lapsed_ in the cor-

C | C/B | **1.** Am7

cy. Her name was Ma-gill,__ And she
ner.

D7 | G7

called her-self Lil,__ but ev-'ry-one knew__ her as Nan-

C | C/B | **2.** **Barrelhouse style** (♩♩ = ♩³♩) Am7

-cy.__ Now *(Instrumental)*

D7

G7 | C

C/B | Am7 | D7sus

Now the doc-tor came in__ stink-ing of gin_

D7 | G7 | C

_ and pro-ceed-ed to lie__ on the ta-ble.

C/B | Am7

He said, "Rock-y, you met_ your match," And Rock-y

said, "Doc, it's on-ly a scratch,_ And I'll be bet-ter, I'll be bet-ter

Doc, as soon_ as I am a - ble." Now

Rock - y Rac - coon, _ he fell back in his room _

on - ly to find _ Gid-eon's Bi - ble.

Gid-eon checked out _ and he left it no doubt _ to

help with good Rock - y's re - vi - val. _

Barrelhouse style

(Instrumental)

SGT. PEPPER'S LONELY HEARTS CLUB BAND

Words and Music by
JOHN LENNON and PAUL McCARTNEY

Moderately slow, but with a strong beat

It was twen-ty years a-go to-day__ Ser-geant
real-ly want to stop the show__ but I

Pep - per taught the band to play__ They've been
thought you might like to know__ that the

go - ing in and out of style,__ but they're
sing - er's going to sing a song,__ and he

guar - an - teed to raise a smile.__ So
wants you all to sing a - long.__ So

may I in - tro - duce to you __ the
let me in - tro - duce to you __ the

act you've known all these years: __ Ser- geant Pep-per's Lone-ly Hearts Club
one and on-ly Bil-ly Shears. __ }

Band. __ (Instrumental)

© 1967 NORTHERN SONGS LTD.
All Rights Controlled and Administered by EMI BLACKWOOD MUSIC INC.
under license from ATV MUSIC CORP. (MACLEN MUSIC)

such a love-ly au-di-ence, we'd like to take you home with us, we'd

love to take you home. I don't Ser-geant Pep-per's Lone-ly Hearts

Club Band, We'd like to thank you once a-gain.

Ser-geant Pep-per's one and on-ly

Lone-ly Hearts Club Band, It's get-ting ver-y near the end.

Ser-geant Pep-per's Lone-ly, Ser-

-geant Pep-per's Lone-ly, Ser-geant Pep-per's Lone-ly Hearts

Club Band.

SHE CAME IN THROUGH THE BATHROOM WINDOW

Words and Music by
JOHN LENNON and PAUL McCARTNEY

She Came In Through The Bath-room Win-dow,
And so I quit the p'lice de-part-ment,

pro-tect-ed by a sil-ver spoon.
and got my-self a stead-y job.

But now she sucks her thumb and won-ders by the
And though she tried her best to help me, she could

banks of her own la-goon. Did-n't an-y-bod-y tell
steal but she could not rob. Did-n't an-y-bod-y tell

her? Did-n't an-y-bod-y see?

© 1969 NORTHERN SONGS LTD.
All Rights Controlled and Administered by EMI BLACKWOOD MUSIC INC.
under license from ATV MUSIC CORP. (MACLEN MUSIC)

193

SHE LOVES YOU

Words and Music by
JOHN LENNON and PAUL McCARTNEY

Copyright © 1963 NORTHERN SONGS LTD.
Copyright Renewed
All rights for the United States of America, its territories and possessions and Canada
assigned to and controlled by GIL MUSIC CORP., 1650 Broadway, New York, NY

195

She said you hurt her so,
know it's up to you,.

She al-most lost her mind. ___ But
I think it's on-ly fair. ___

now she says she knows___ You're not the hurt-ing
Pride can hurt you too ___ A-pol-o-gize to

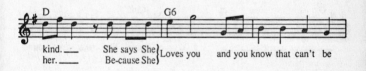

kind. ___ She says She } Loves you and you know that can't be
her. ___ Be-cause She }

bad. Yes, She Loves You and you

know you should be glad. _____ oo! ___ She

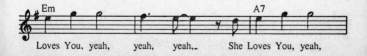

Loves You, yeah, yeah, yeah,_ She Loves You, yeah,

SHE'S LEAVING HOME

Words and Music by
JOHN LENNON and PAUL McCARTNEY

Moderately

E   Bm   F#m7

Wedn's - day morn - ing at five o' -
Fa - ther snores as his wife gets

C#m7

clock as the day be - gins ___
in - to her dress - ing gown ___

F#7   B11

Si - lent - ly clos - ing her
Picks up the let - ter that's

B9   B11

bed - room door ___ Leav - ing the
ly - ing there ___ Stand - ing a -

B9

note that she hoped would say more She goes
lone at the top of the stairs She breaks

% E   Bm   F#m7

down - stairs to the kit - chen
down and cries to her hus - band
Fri - day morn - ing at nine o' -

© 1967 NORTHERN SONGS LTD.
All Rights Controlled and Administered by EMI BLACKWOOD MUSIC INC.
under license from ATV MUSIC CORP. (MACLEN MUSIC)

198

(We gave her ev-'ry-thing money could)
(We strug-gled hard all our lives to get
(Fun is the one thing that mo-ney can't

She's Leav-ing Home af-ter liv-ing a-
by

lone for so man-y years
Bye - bye)

1. F#9
2. F#9 D.S. al Coda

CODA
Some-thing in-
buy

side that was al-ways de-nied for so man-y years
(Bye - bye)

She's leav-ing

home Bye - bye.

SHE'S A WOMAN

Words and Music by
JOHN LENNON and PAUL McCARTNEY

Fairly bright, with a strong back beat

My love don't give me pres - ents,
She don't give boys the eye. __

I know that she's no peas-ant.
She hates to see me cry. __

On - ly ev - er has __
She is hap - py just __

__ to give me love for - ev - er and for - ev - er;
__ to hear me say that I will nev - er leave her;

My love don't give me pres - ents.
She don't give boys the eye. __

Turn me on __ when I __ get lone - ly,
She will nev - er make __ me jeal - ous,

Peo - ple tell me that she's on - ly fool - in', I
Gives me all her time as well as lov - in', Don't

© 1964 NORTHERN SONGS LTD.
Copyright Renewed
All Rights Controlled and Administered by EMI BLACKWOOD MUSIC INC.
under license from ATV MUSIC CORP. (MACLEN MUSIC)

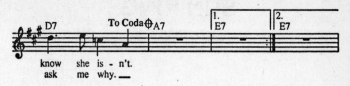

know   she   is - n't.
ask   me   why. __

She's   A   Wom - an   who   un - der - stands; __

She's   A   Wom - an   who   loves her   man. __

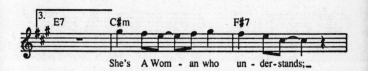

She's   A Wom - an who   un - der - stands; __

She's   A   Wom - an   who   loves her   man. __

CODA

She's   A   Wom -

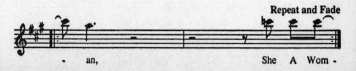

Repeat and Fade

- an,   She   A   Wom -

SUN KING

Words and Music by
JOHN LENNON and PAUL McCARTNEY

© 1969 NORTHERN SONGS LTD.
All Rights Controlled and Administered by EMI BLACKWOOD MUSIC INC.
under license from ATV MUSIC CORP. (MACLEN MUSIC)

Here comes the Sun King.

Quan - do __ pa - ra mu - cho __ mi a -

mor - e __ de fe - li - ce __ cor - a -

zon. Mun - do __ pa - pa - raz - zi __ mi a -

mor - e __ chick-a fer - dy __ pa - ra sol.

Cues - to __ ob - ri - ga - do __ tan - ta

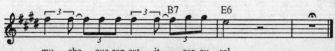

mu - cho __ que can eat it __ car - ou - sel.

SOMETHING

Words and Music by
GEORGE HARRISON

Slowly

(Instrumental)

Some-thing in the way she moves,
Some-where in her smile she knows
Some-thing in the way she knows,

at - tracts me like no oth-er lov - er.
that I don't need no oth-er lov - er.
and all I have to do is think of her.

Some-thing in the way she woos me.
Some-thing in her style that shows me.
Some-thing in the things she shows me.

To Coda

don't want to leave her now, you know I be-lieve and how.

1.
(Instrumental)

2.
(Instrumental)

You're ask-ing me will my love grow, I don't know.

© 1969 HARRISONGS LTD.

STRAWBERRY FIELDS FOREVER

Words and Music by
JOHN LENNON and PAUL McCARTNEY

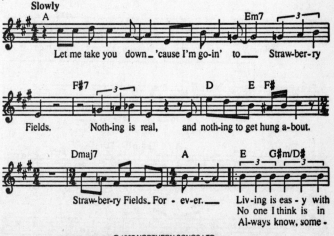

© 1967 NORTHERN SONGS LTD.
All Rights Controlled and Administered by EMI BLACKWOOD MUSIC INC.
under license from ATV MUSIC CORP. (MACLEN MUSIC)

eyes closed,__ Mis-un-der-stand-ing all you see.__
my tree__ I mean it must be high or low.__
time think it's me, But you know I know when it's a dream.__

It's get-ting hard to be some-one but it all__ works__out,
That is, you know you can't tune in but it's all_____ right
I think a "No" will be a "Yes," but it's all_____ wrong

it does-n't mat-ter much to me.)
that is, I think it's not too bad.}   Let me take you down__
that is, I think I dis-a-gree.)

__ 'cause I'm go-ing to__ Straw-ber-ry Fields.

Noth-ing is real, and noth-ing to get hung a-bout...

1.,2.

Straw-ber-ry Fields__ For - ev - er. __

3.

Straw-ber-ry Fields__ For - ev-er,__ Straw-ber-ry Fields__ For -

ev-er,__ Straw-ber-ry Fields__ For - ev-er. __

TICKET TO RIDE

Words and Music by
JOHN LENNON and PAUL McCARTNEY

Moderate Rock tempo

(Instrumental)

I think I'm gon - na be sad,
said that liv - ing with me

I think it's to - day yeah!
is bring - in' her down yeah!

The girl that's driv - ing me mad
For she would nev - er be free

Bm7   E7

is go - ing a - way.
when I was a - round.

F#m   D7

She's got a Tick - et To Ride,

© 1965 NORTHERN SONGS LTD.
Copyright Renewed
All Rights Controlled and Administered by EMI BLACKWOOD MUSIC INC.
under license from ATV MUSIC CORP. (MACLEN MUSIC)

She's got a Tick-et To Ri - hi - hide, __

She's got a Tick-et To Ride, __ but she don't care! __

1. A __ 2. A She __

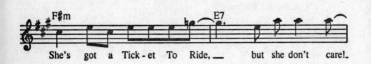

I don't know why she's rid - in' so high, __

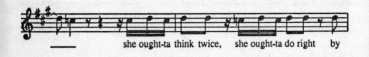

__ she ought-ta think twice, she ought-ta do right by

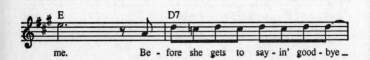

me. Be - fore she gets to say - in' good - bye __

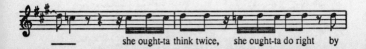

__ she ought-ta think twice, she ought-ta do right by

me.

E   A

1. { I think I'm gon-na be sad,
2. { She said that liv-ing with me

The girl that's driv-ing me mad
For she would nev-er be free

Bm7   E7

is go-ing a-way. { Yeah!
when I was a-round. }   Oh,

F#m   D7

she's got a Tick-et To Ride.

F#m   G

She's got a Tick-et To Ri - hi - hide,

F#m   E7   1. A

She's got a Tick-et To Ride, but she don't care!

2. A   Repeat and Fade

I   My ba-by don't care!

TAXMAN

Words and Music by
GEORGE HARRISON

Moderate Rock

Let me — tell you — how it — will be: —
— per - cent ap - pear — too small, —
(See additional lyrics)

There's one — for you, — nine - teen — for me. —
Be thank - ful I — don't take — it all. —

'Cause I'm the Tax - man,

To Coda ⊕

Yeah, — I'm the — Tax - man.

1.,3. | 2.

If you drive — a car, — car;

Should five.
Now my —

I'll tax —

If you try — to sit, — sit; —

— the street;

I'll tax —

© 1966 NORTHERN SONGS LTD.
All Rights Controlled and Administered by EMI BLACKWOOD MUSIC INC.
under license from ATV MUSIC CORP. (MACLEN MUSIC)

Additional Verses

3. Don't ask me what I want it for,
   If you don't want to pay some more.
   'Cause I'm the taxman,
   Yeah, I'm the taxman.

4. Now my advice for those who die,
   Declare the pennies on your eyes,
   'Cause I'm the taxman,
   Yeah, I'm the taxman.

TELL ME
WHAT YOU SEE

Words and Music by
JOHN LENNON and PAUL McCARTNEY

Medium tempo

1. If you let me take your heart
2. Big and black the clouds may be
3. Lis-ten to me one more time

I will prove to you
Time will pass a - way
How can I get through?

We will nev - er be a - part,
If you put your trust in me,
Can't you try to see that I'm,

If I'm part of you.
I'll make bright your day.
Try - in' to get to you?

O - pen up your eyes now,
Look in - to these eyes now,
O - pen up your eyes now,

© 1965 NORTHERN SONGS LTD.
Copyright Renewed
All Rights Controlled and Administered by EMI BLACKWOOD MUSIC INC.
under license from ATV MUSIC CORP. (MACLEN MUSIC)

TELL ME WHY

Words and Music by
JOHN LENNON and PAUL McCARTNEY

Brightly

(Instrumental)

Tell Me Why _____ you cried _____ and why you lied _____ to me. _____ Tell Me Why _____ you cried, _____ and why you lied _____ to me.

{ 1. Well, I gave _____ you ev-'ry-thing I had, _____ But you left me sit-ting on my own. _____ Did you have _____ to treat me oh so bad? _____ All I

{ 2. If it's some- thing that I've said or done, _____ Tell me what, and I'll a-pol-o-gize. _____ If you don't. I real-ly can't go on. _____ Hold-ing

© 1964 NORTHERN SONGS LTD.
Copyright Renewed
All Rights Controlled and Administered by EMI BLACKWOOD MUSIC INC.
under license from ATV MUSIC CORP. (MACLEN MUSIC)

THERE'S A PLACE

Words and Music by
JOHN LENNON and PAUL McCARTNEY

Moderately bright

There _____ is a place

where I can go when I feel

low, when I feel blue.

And it's my mind, _____ and there's no

time _____ when I'm a - lone. _____

I _____ think of

you and things you do

© Copyright 1964 NORTHERN SONGS
All rights for the United States of America and its territories and possession and Canada
assigned to and controlled by GIL MUSIC CORP., 1650 Broadway, New York, NY 10019

THINGS WE
SAID TODAY

Words and Music by
JOHN LENNON and PAUL McCARTNEY

Moderately fast

You say you will love me if I have to go,
You say you'll be mine, girl, 'til the end of time,

You'll be think-ing of me
These days such a kind, girl,

some-how I will know.
seems so hard to find.

Some-day when I'm
Some-day when we're

lone-ly wish-ing you weren't so far a-way,
dream-ing deep in love, not a lot to say,

Then I will re-mem-ber Things We Said To-day.
Then we will re-mem-ber Things We Said To-day.

1. Me, I'm just the luck-

2.

y kind, Love to hear you say that love is love.

© 1964 NORTHERN SONGS LTD.
Copyright Renewed
All Rights Controlled and Administered by EMI BLACKWOOD MUSIC INC.
under license from ATV MUSIC CORP. (MACLEN MUSIC)

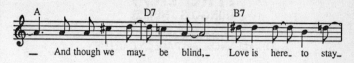

And though we may be blind, Love is here to stay

and that's e - nough to make you mine girl,

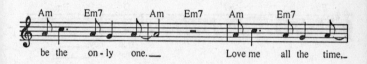

be the on - ly one. Love me all the time,

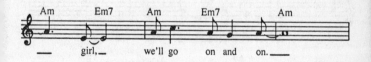

girl, we'll go on and on.

Some-day when we're dream - ing, deep in love not a

lot to say, Then we will re - mem - ber

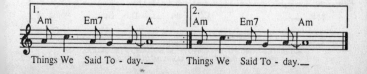

1.
Things We Said To - day.

2.
Things We Said To - day.

THIS BOY
(RINGO'S THEME)

Words and Music by
JOHN LENNON and PAUL McCARTNEY

© 1963, 1964 NORTHERN SONGS LTD.
Copyright Renewed
All Rights Controlled and Administered by EMI BLACKWOOD MUSIC INC.
under license from ATV MUSIC CORP. (MACLEN MUSIC)

TWO OF US

Words and Music by
JOHN LENNON and PAUL McCARTNEY

Brightly, in 2

Two Of Us, rid - ing no - where,
Two Of Us, send - ing post - cards,
Two Of Us, wear - ing rain - coats,

spend - ing some - one's hard - earned
writ - ing let - ters, on my
stand - ing so - lo, in the

pay. You and me, Sun - day driv -
wall. You and me, burn - ing match -
sun. You and me, chas - ing pa -

- ing, not ar - riv - ing
- es, lift - ing latch - es
- per, get - ting no - where

on our way back
on our way back
on our way back

home.
home.
home.
We're on our way

© 1969, 1970 NORTHERN SONGS LTD.
All Rights Controlled and Administered by EMI BLACKWOOD MUSIC INC.
under license from ATV MUSIC CORP. (MACLEN MUSIC)

home, We're on our way home.

We're go-in' home.

You and I

have mem - o - ries

long - er than the road that stretch -

- es out a - head.

(Instrumental)

(Spoken:) We're go in' home.   Better believe it. Goodbye.

TWIST AND SHOUT

Words and Music by
BERT RUSSELL and PHIL MEDLEY

Moderately, with a beat

Well, shake it up ba - by, now.___ (Shake it up ba-

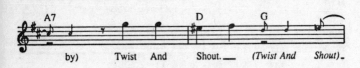

by) Twist And Shout.___ (Twist And Shout)

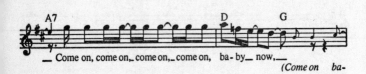

_ Come on, come on,_ come on,_ come on, ba-by_ now,___ (Come on ba-

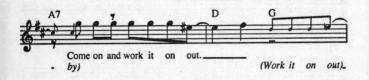

Come on and work it on out.___ (Work it on out)_
- by) (Work it on out)_

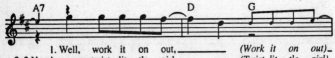

1. Well, work it on out,_____ (Work it on out)_
2.,3. You know you twist, lit - tle girl,_____ (Twist lit - tle girl)_

© 1960 (Renewed 1988) SCREEN GEMS-EMI MUSIC INC.,
UNICHAPPELL MUSIC INC. and SLOOPY II, INC.
All Rights for UNICHAPPELL MUSIC INC. in the U.S.
Controlled and Administered by SCREEN GEMS-EMI MUSIC INC.
All Rights outside the U.S. Controlled and Administered by SCREEN GEMS-EMI MUSIC INC.

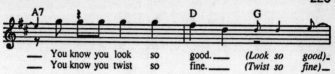

— You know you look so good.— *(Look so good).*
— You know you twist so fine.— *(Twist so fine)*—

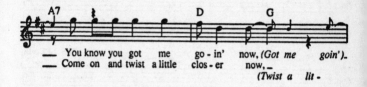

— You know you got me go-in' now, *(Got me goin').*—
— Come on and twist a little clos-er now,— *(Twist a lit-*

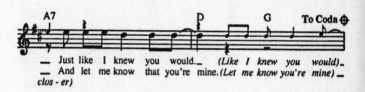

To Coda ⊕

— Just like I knew you would.— *(Like I knew you would)*—
— And let me know that you're mine. *(Let me know you're mine)* —
clos-er)

1. A7   2. A7

— Well, shake it up ba-—

(Instrumental)

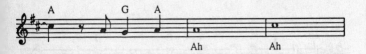

Ah   Ah

Ah   Ah   Ah _____   Shake it up ba-

D.S. al Coda

CODA

_ Well, shake it, shake it, shake it,   ba-by,   now, _____
(Shake it up ba-

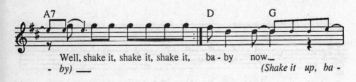

Well, shake it, shake it, shake it,   ba-by   now._
- *by)* _   *(Shake it up, ba-*

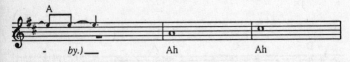

- *by.)* _   Ah   Ah

Ah   Ah
(Instrumental)

WHEN I'M SIXTY-FOUR

Words and Music by
JOHN LENNON and PAUL McCARTNEY

© 1967 NORTHERN SONGS LTD.
All Rights Controlled and Administered by EMI BLACKWOOD MUSIC INC.
under license from ATV MUSIC CORP. (MACLEN MUSIC)

Am · E

You'll be old-er, too.

Am

Ah, _____ and if you

Dm · F · G

say the word _____ I could stay with

C · G

you. *(Instrumental)*

%C

I could be hand - y mend - ing a fuse _____
Send me a post - card, drop me a line _____

G7

when your lights have gone. _____
stat - ing point of view. _____

You can knit a sweat - er by the fire - side, _____
In - di - cate pre - cise - ly what you mean to say _____

N.C. · C

Sun - day morn - ing go for a ride. _____
Your sin - cere - ly wast - ing a - way. _____

Do - ing the gar - den, dig - ging the weeds, _____
Give me your an - swer, fill in a form, _____

Who could ask for more?
Mine for - ev - er more.

Will you still need me,
will you still feed me, When I'm Six - ty Four?

Ev' - ry sum - mer we can rent a cot - tage in the Isle of Wight

— if it's not too dear. — We shall

scrimp and save; _____

Grand - chil - dren on your knee; ___ Ve - ra,

Chuck and Dave. *(Instrumental)*

D.S. al Coda

CODA

Four? Ho! *(Instrumental)*

WE CAN WORK IT OUT

Words and Music by
JOHN LENNON and PAUL McCARTNEY

© 1965 NORTHERN SONGS LTD.
Copyright Renewed
All Rights Controlled and Administered by EMI BLACKWOOD MUSIC INC.
under license from ATV MUSIC CORP. (MACLEN MUSIC)

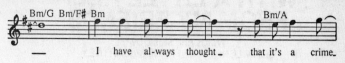

I have al-ways thought — that it's a crime —

so I will ask you once a-

gain. Try so see it my way,

on-ly time will tell if I am right or I am wrong.

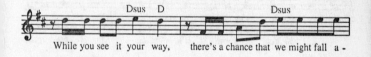

While you see it your way, there's a chance that we might fall a-

part be-fore too long. We Can Work It Out,

We Can Work It Out. — (Instrumental)

WITH A LITTLE HELP FROM MY FRIENDS

Words and Music by
JOHN LENNON and PAUL McCARTNEY

© 1967 NORTHERN SONGS LTD.
All Rights Controlled and Administered by EMI BLACKWOOD MUSIC INC.
under license from ATV MUSIC CORP. (MACLEN MUSIC)

1.
E   B7

With A Lit-tle Help From My Friends._
With A Lit-tle Help From My Friends._
With A Lit-tle Help From My Friends.

2., 3.
E   C#m   F#7

_   (Do you   need_   an-y-bod - y?)   I
_   (Do you   need_   an-y-bod - y?)   I

E   D   A   C#m

need some-bod - y to love._ (Could it   be_   an-y-bod-
just need some-one to love._ (Could it   be_   an-y-bod-

D.C. al Coda
(3rd ending)
F#7   E   D   To Coda ⊕ A

- y?)   I   want some-bod-y to love. _
- y?)   I   want some-bod-y to love._

CODA
⊕   A   D   A

_   Oh, I get by_ With A Lit-tle Help_ From My Friends._

E   D   A

_   Mm, I'm gon-na try_ With A Lit-tle Help_ From My Friends._

E   A

_   Oh, I get high_ With A Lit-tle Help_ From My Friends._

E   D

_   Yes, I get by_ With A Lit-tle Help_ From My Friends._

A   C/G   Am6   E

With A Lit-tle Help From My Friends._

WHILE MY GUITAR GENTLY WEEPS

Words and Music by
GEORGE HARRISON

© 1968 HARRISONGS LTD.

Still my gui-tar ___ gen-tly weeps. ___

I ___ don't know why ___
I ___ don't know why ___

no - bod - y told ___ you   how   to un-
you ___ were di-vert - ed,   you ___ were per-

fold ___   your   love. ___
vert - ed,   too. ___

I   don't know   how ___
I   don't know   how ___

some - one con-trolled you, ___   they ___ bought and
you ___ were in - vert - ed, ___   no ___ one a-

sold ___   you. ___   I   look ___
lert - ed   you. ___   I   look ___

___ at ___ the world. ___   and I   no - tice ___ it's turn-
___ at ___ you all, ___   see the love ___ there ___ that's sleep-

236

YOU NEVER GIVE ME
YOUR MONEY

Words and Music by
JOHN LENNON and PAUL McCARTNEY

Slowly

(Instrumental)

You Nev-er Give Me Your
I nev-er give you my

Mon - ey, ___ You on - ly give me your
num - ber, ___ I on - ly give you my

fun - ny pa - per, And in the mid-dle of ne -
sit - u - a - tion, And in the mid-dle of in -

go - ti - a - tions you break down. ___
ves - ti - ga - tion I break down. ___

© 1969 NORTHERN SONGS LTD.
All Rights Controlled and Administered by EMI BLACKWOOD MUSIC INC.
under license from ATV MUSIC CORP. (MACLEN MUSIC)

One sweet dream.

Pick up the bags and get in the lim - ou - sine

Soon we'll be a - way from here

Step on the gas and wipe that tear a - way One sweet dream

came true to - day came true

to - day.

Repeat and Fade

One, two, three, four, five, six, sev - en, All good chil - dren go to heav - en.

YELLOW SUBMARINE

Words and Music by
JOHN LENNON and PAUL McCARTNEY

March tempo

In the town ___ where I was born lived a man ___ who sailed to sea. And he told ___ us of his life in the land ___ of sub-mar-ines. So we sailed ___ up to the sun till we found ___ the sea of green. And we lived ___ be-neath the waves in our Yel-low Sub-mar-ine. We all live in a Yel-low Sub-mar-ine,

© 1966 NORTHERN SONGS LTD.
All Rights Controlled and Administered by EMI BLACKWOOD MUSIC INC.
under license from ATV MUSIC CORP. (MACLEN MUSIC)

Yel - low Sub - mar-ine, Yel - low Sub - mar-ine.

We all live in a Yel - low Sub - mar-ine,

Yel - low Sub - mar-ine, Yel - low Sub - mar-ine. { And our / As we

friends ____ are all on board, man - y
live ____ a life of ease, ev - 'ry

more of them live next door. And the
one of us has all we need. Sky of

band ____ be-gins to play; *(Instrumental)*
blue ____ and sea of

green in our Yel - low . Sub - mar-ine.

YESTERDAY

Words and Music by
JOHN LENNON and PAUL McCARTNEY

Moderately, with expression

Yes-ter-day, ___ all my trou-bles seemed so
Sud-den-ly, ___ I'm not half the man I

far a-way, ___ Now it looks as though they're
used to be, ___ There's a shad-ow hang - ing

here to stay, ___ oh I be - lieve ___ in
o - ver me, ___ oh Yes-ter-day ___ came

Yes - ter - day. ___
sud - den - ly. ___ Why she had to go I don't

know. she would-n't say. ___ I said

some-thing wrong, now I long for Yes-ter-day.

© 1965 NORTHERN SONGS LTD.
Copyright Renewed
All Rights Controlled and Administered by EMI BLACKWOOD MUSIC INC.
under license from ATV MUSIC CORP. (MACLEN MUSIC)

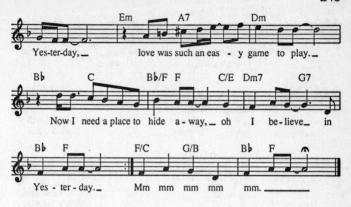

Yes-ter-day, __ love was such an eas - y game to play. __

Now I need a place to hide a-way, __ oh I be-lieve __ in

Yes - ter-day. __ Mm mm mm mm mm. __

YOU WON'T SEE ME

Words and Music by
JOHN LENNON and PAUL McCARTNEY

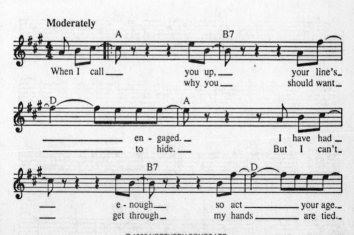

Moderately

When I call __ you up, __ your line's
why you __ should want

__ en - gaged. __ I have had __
__ to hide. __ But I can't __

__ e - nough __ so act __ your age. __
__ get through __ my hands __ are tied. __

© 1965 NORTHERN SONGS LTD.
Copyright Renewed
All Rights Controlled and Administered by EMI BLACKWOOD MUSIC INC.
under license from ATV MUSIC CORP. (MACLEN MUSIC)

YOU'RE GOING TO LOSE THAT GIRL

Words and Music by
JOHN LENNON and PAUL McCARTNEY

You're gon-na lose that girl,— You're gon-na

lose that girl.——— If you don't take her
If you don't treat her

out to-night,— she's gon-na change her mind.—
right my friend,— you're gon-na find her gone.—

And I will take her
'Cause I will treat her

out to-night— and I will treat her kind.—
right and then— you'll be the lone-ly one.—

You're gon-na lose that girl — You're gon-na

© 1965 NORTHERN SONGS LTD.
Copyright Renewed
All Rights Controlled and Administered by EMI BLACKWOOD MUSIC INC.
under license from ATV MUSIC CORP. (MACLEN MUSIC)

YOU'VE GOT TO HIDE YOUR LOVE AWAY

Words and Music by
JOHN LENNON and PAUL McCARTNEY

Here I stand head in hand, turn my face to the
How can I e-ven try? I can nev-er

wall. If she's gone I can't go on
win. Hear-ing them, see-ing them

feel-ing two foot small.
in the state I'm in.

Ev-'ry-where peo-ple stare each and ev-'ry
How could she say to me "Love will find a

day. I can see them laugh at me
way?" Gath-er 'round all you clowns,

And I hear them say:
let me hear you say:

"Hey, You've Got To Hide Your Love A-way!"

© 1965 NORTHERN SONGS LTD.
Copyright Renewed
All Rights Controlled and Administered by EMI BLACKWOOD MUSIC INC.
under license from ATV MUSIC CORP. (MACLEN MUSIC)

"Hey, You've Got To Hide Your Love A - way!"

(Instrumental)

YOUR MOTHER SHOULD KNOW

Words and Music by
JOHN LENNON and PAUL McCARTNEY

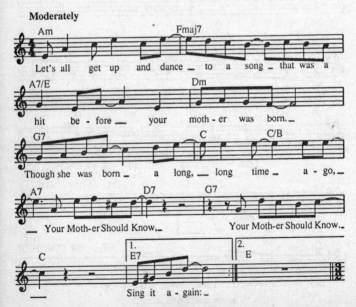

Moderately

Let's all get up and dance to a song that was a

hit be - fore your moth - er was born.

Though she was born a long, long time a - go,

Your Moth-er Should Know, Your Moth-er Should Know.

Sing it a - gain:

© 1967 COMET MUSIC CORP.
All Rights Controlled and Administered by EMI APRIL MUSIC INC.
under license from WELBECK MUSIC CORP. (COMET)

251

GUITAR CHORD FRAMES

	C	Cm	C+	C6	Cm6
C					

	C#	C#m	C#+	C#6	C#m6
C#/Db					

	D	Dm	D+	D6	Dm6
D					

	Eb	Ebm	Eb+	Eb6	Ebm6
Eb/D#					

	E	Em	E+	E6	Em6
E					

	F	Fm	F+	F6	Fm6
F					

This guitar chord reference includes 120 commonly used chords. For a more complete guide to guitar chords, see "THE PAPERBACK CHORD BOOK" (HL00702009).

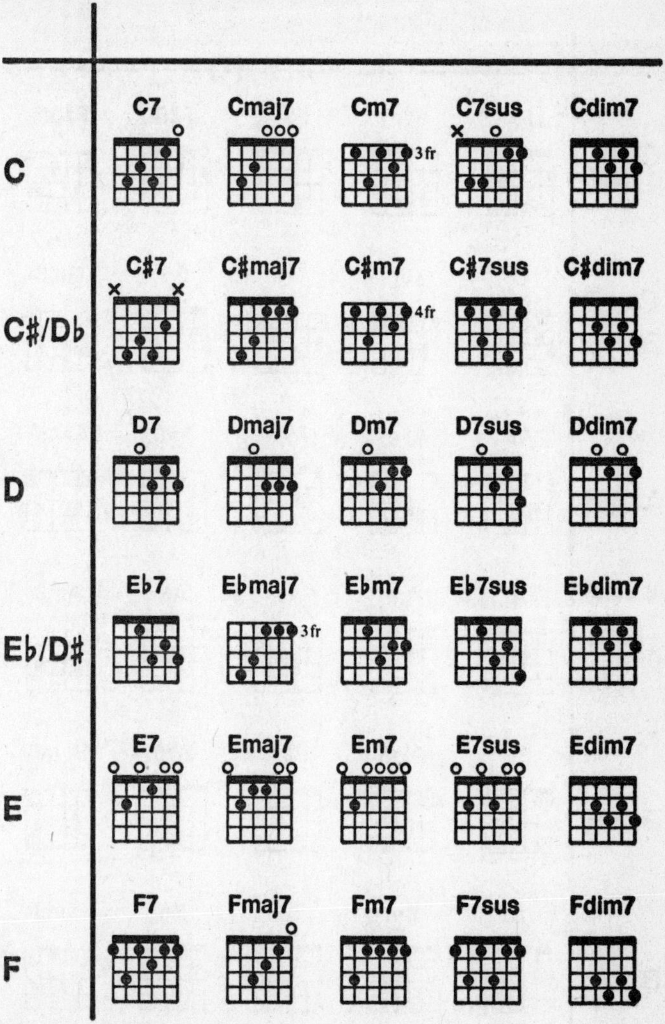
C
C7
Cmaj7
Cm7
3 fr
C7sus
Cdim7
C#/D♭
C#7
C#maj7
C#m7
4 fr
C#7sus
C#dim7
D
D7
Dmaj7
Dm7
D7sus
Ddim7
E♭/D#
E♭7
E♭maj7
3 fr
E♭m7
E♭7sus
E♭dim7
E
E7
Emaj7
Em7
E7sus
Edim7
F
F7
Fmaj7
Fm7
F7sus
Fdim7

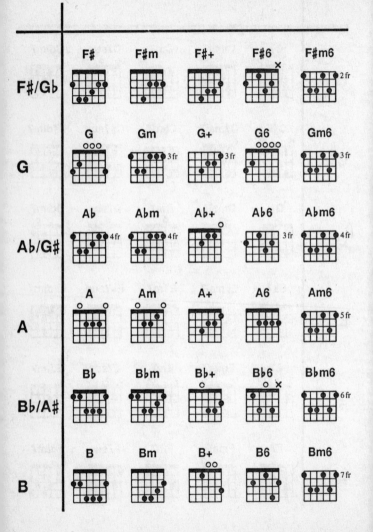

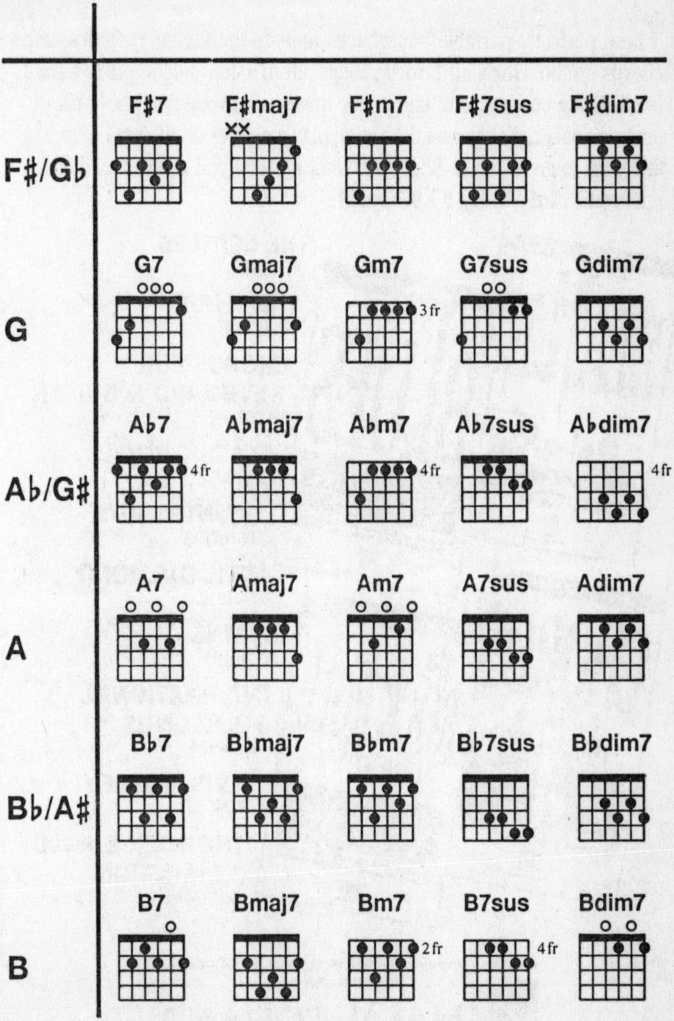
F♯/G♭
F♯7 F♯maj7 F♯m7 F♯7sus F♯dim7
G
G7 Gmaj7 Gm7 G7sus Gdim7
3 fr
A♭/G♯
A♭7 A♭maj7 A♭m7 A♭7sus A♭dim7
4 fr
A
A7 Amaj7 Am7 A7sus Adim7
B♭/A♯
B♭7 B♭maj7 B♭m7 B♭7sus B♭dim7
B
B7 Bmaj7 Bm7 B7sus Bdim7
2 fr
4 fr

THE PAPERBACK SONGS SERIES

These perfectly portable paperbacks include the melodies, lyrics, and chords symbols for your favorite songs, all in a convenient, pocket-sized book. Using concise, one-line music notation, anyone from hobbyists to professionals can strum on the guitar, play melodies on the piano, or sing the lyrics to great songs. Books also include a helpful guitar chord chart. A fantastic deal – **only $5.95 each!**

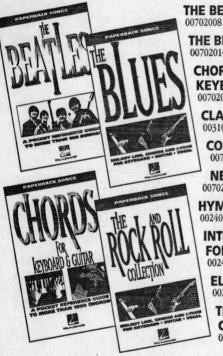

THE BEATLES
00702008

THE BLUES
00702014

CHORDS FOR KEYBOARD & GUITAR
00702009

CLASSIC ROCK
00310058

COUNTRY HITS
00702013

NEIL DIAMOND
00702012

HYMNS
00240103

INTERNATIONAL FOLKSONGS
00240104

ELVIS PRESLEY
00240102

THE ROCK & ROLL COLLECTION
00702020

FOR MORE INFORMATION, SEE YOUR LOCAL MUSIC DEALER,
OR WRITE TO:

HAL • LEONARD®
CORPORATION
7777 W. BLUEMOUND RD. P.O. BOX 13819 MILWAUKEE, WI 53213

Prices, availability and contents subject to change without notice.
Some products may not be available outside the U.S.A.